PATHWAYS to POWER:
KEYS THAT OPEN DOORS

Paul N. Tassell, Ph. D.

REGULAR BAPTIST PRESS
1300 North Meacham Road
Schaumburg, Illinois 60173-4888

INTRODUCTION

In chapter 11 of his second letter to the Corinthians, the apostle Paul mentioned the many perils he faced in his ministry. They were real and varied as the great missionary to the Gentiles crisscrossed the world of his day to establish and strengthen scores of churches and believers.

The present day has its perils too. Those who love the truth and have been called of God to His service are well aware of this fact, but perhaps no one has the chance to get a better overview of these problems and needs than someone who, not unlike the apostle Paul, travels up and down the country and into other lands ministering to churches. Dr. Paul N. Tassell, who began his work as National Representative of the General Association of Regular Baptist Churches in 1979, has preached in churches in practically every state of the Union. Certainly there is no better way to ascertain the needs and dangers facing a fellowship than this extensive personal contact.

Whether the reader is a servant of the Lord starting out in his ministry, a layman wanting to learn more about the unique stand of the GARBC or a seasoned man of God reviewing what our mind should be concerning present-day issues, this volume will be valuable. With Dr. Tassell's experience as a former pastor and a counselor to pastors, the reader will sense the warmth of a pastor's heart, the urgency of a pastor's warnings and solutions from a pastor's godly wisdom.

>	Norman A. Olson
>	Book Editor and
>	Managing Editor, the
>	*Baptist Bulletin*

Library of Congress Cataloging in Publication Data

Tassell, Paul N., 1934—
  Pathways to power.

    1. Regular Baptists—Doctrinal and controversial works.
I.   Title.
BX6388.37.T37   1983   230'.61   83-9576
ISBN 0-87227-093-9

© 1983
Regular Baptist Press
Schaumburg, Illinois
Printed in U.S.A.
All rights reserved

Second printing—1992

Contents

Preface 7
1. Keys That Open Doors 9
2. Evangelism 15
3. Demonism and Exorcism 23
4. The Primacy of Preaching 31
5. Reincarnation or Resurrection? 39
6. Pastoral Perils 47
7. Biblical Separation 57
8. New Evangelicalism 65
9. The Work of the Pulpit Committee 75
10. The Place of the Sunday School 85
11. Evangelistic Outreach, Not Politics 93
12. A Look at Mariolatry 103
13. The Hole and the Hewing—Our Heritage 113
14. Marriage and Divorce 125
15. A Great Door and Effectual Is Opened 133

Preface

Baptists are not "freethinking" according to the traditional definition of that term. Our thoughts are bounded by, grounded in, and founded upon the written Word of God. However, we are free to think! And we do think. *Pathways to Power: Keys That Open Doors* is the fruit of one man's thinking, experience and research. No Baptist leader may rightly profess to speak *ex-cathedra*. Baptists do not believe in papal bulls. We do believe in Bible-based convictions; moreover, we respond positively to expositions and expressions that are truly rooted in the Word of God.

This book has to do with the perspective of *a preacher*. One old sage said: "A preacher ought to love precepts and people." I like to say it another way: A shepherd ought to love the Scriptures and the sheep. Such Spirit-engendered love is, I trust, evident throughout the pages of this volume. I have written because I want to be helpful to God's people. The reader may at times disagree with some point or conclusion, but if I can provoke each reader to think more carefully, pray more fervently and serve our Savior more zealously, my work shall have been amply rewarded.

1

Keys That Open Doors

MANY PEOPLE THINK that all ants do is go to picnics. But these little insects are some of the world's greatest teachers. God's Word says: "Go to the ant, thou sluggard; consider her ways, and be wise: which having no guide, overseer, or ruler, provideth her meat in the summer, and gathereth her food in the harvest" (Prov. 6:6–8). You may go to a picnic to relax, but ants go there to work. Proverbs 30:25 reads: "The ants are a people not strong, yet they prepare their meat in the summer." Summertime is not vacation time for ants; it is work time, harvesttime, production time.

The Bible, in a number of passages, refers to summertime as harvesttime. One such verse is Proverbs 10:5, where we read: "He that gathereth in summer is a wise son: but he that sleepeth in harvest is a son that causeth shame." The summer months are production months. If we fail to work, the crops are lost. Summer in the Bible, therefore, speaks of production and harvest.

According to the Lord Jesus Christ, the most important harvest is not corn or soybeans or wheat. Strange as it may sound, the greatest crop in the world is the soul-crop. Jesus said: "The field is the world" (Matt. 13:38). That field today contains approximately five billion people, five billion never-dying souls who will spend eternity in Heaven or hell. Who will reap the soul-crop? You can be sure the devil is busy in this summer season called time as he seeks to take millions of souls to hell for eternity. The question is: What are you and I as true Christians doing in this summertime of grace to reach the harvest fields of the world with the gospel of Christ?

The one Person Who best instructs us about the harvest is Christ Himself. Matthew tells us, "But when [Jesus] saw the multitudes, he was moved with compassion on them, because they fainted and were scattered abroad, as sheep having no shepherd. Then saith he unto his disciples, The harvest truly is plenteous, but the labourers are few; pray ye therefore the Lord of the harvest, that he will send forth labourers into his harvest" (Matt. 9:36-38). This passage of Scripture reveals a very perplexing situation: a plentiful harvest but a pitiful labor force. The harvest is great, but the laborers are few.

Secularism and materialism are being espoused by millions. The population of the world will number over six billion by the year 2000, and agnostic and atheistic forces are stronger than ever! How can we save the harvest from hell? How can we reap the millions of souls for God and Heaven? How can we best invest the summertime of our lives in work that will count for all of eternity?

In Matthew 9:38 Jesus gives the answer. He gives us four keys to unlocking the hearts of people for God. Let us consider them carefully, and as ants at a picnic, let us be diligent in putting them to work. "Only one life, 'twill soon be past. Only what's done for Christ will last." In view of the urgency of the times in which we live, let us listen to the Word of our Lord carefully.

The Key Procedure

The first step in our summer success has to do with the key procedure. Jesus said, "Pray ye." Prayer is the initial implementation of fulfilling the Great Commission. And yet prayerlessness may well be the most prevailing sin to be found among God's people. Jesus said: "Men ought always to pray, and not to faint" (Luke 18:1). The implication is quite clear: If you are spiritually faint, you are probably not praying as you ought. Paul wrote: "Pray without ceasing" (1 Thess. 5:17). Jesus declares: "The effectual fervent prayer of a righteous man availeth much" (James 5:16). Prayer produces. Prayer prevails. The believer must pray for souls, for soul-winners.

Our churches need to be houses of prayer. We need to be praying that God would call our young people into service for the winning of souls and the building of New Testament local churches around the world.

Prayer is the key procedure. Mighty men of God of the past have perceived this and practiced it. Dwight L. Moody said, "The church of Jesus Christ must go forward on her knees." The sad truth is that too many Christians wear out the seats of their pants before the knees. We too often are "sitting on the premises instead of standing on the promises." The great New York City pastor of another generation, J. H. Jowett, declared, "I would rather teach one man to pray than to teach ten men to preach." And, yet, too often men come out of our seminaries knowing how to talk to men about God but not having learned to talk to God about men. It was said of Charles Haddon Spurgeon that he seldom went more than ten minutes without praying. Our public performance can only be effective when our private praying is what it ought to be.

The Key Person

The key **procedure,** prayer, is in partnership with the key **Person.** Jesus said: "Pray ye therefore the Lord of the harvest." Who is the Lord of the harvest? It is vital that we know, for He is the key Person in properly investing the summertime of our lives. For His identity we go to the book of Acts, chapter 13, verses 2 through 5: "As they ministered to the Lord, and fasted, the Holy Ghost said, Separate me Barnabas and Saul for the work whereunto I have called them. And when they had fasted and prayed, and laid their hands on them, they sent them away. So they, being sent forth by the Holy Ghost, departed unto Seleucia." This passage of Scripture makes it clear that the Holy Spirit is the Lord of the harvest.

The Holy Spirit commanded the setting apart of Barnabas and Saul. According to the Word of God, those two first-century missionaries were "sent forth by the Holy Spirit." This ministry of the Holy Spirit as Lord of the harvest is perfectly in keeping with the last words of Christ to His disciples as recorded in Acts 1:8: "But ye shall receive power, after that the Holy Ghost is come upon you: and ye shall be witnesses unto me both in Jerusalem, and in all Judaea, and in Samaria, and unto the uttermost part of the earth." The Holy Spirit is concerned with taking the Gospel of Jesus Christ to all the world.

Jesus said: "But when the Comforter is come, whom I will send unto you from the Father, even the Spirit of truth, which proceedeth from the Father, he shall testify of me: and ye also shall bear witness" (John 15:26, 27). Some people mistakenly believe that the Holy Spirit's main ministry is one of emotional stimulation or spectacular gifts. Such is not the case. The Holy Spirit is primarily interested in empowering believers to tell others the gospel of Christ. If we are to be effective in harvesting souls, we must work in the energy of the Spirit of God and according to the Word of God. We are reminded in Zechariah 4:6: "Not by might, nor by power, but by my spirit, saith the LORD of hosts."

The Key Program

Listen again to the words of Proverbs 10:5: "He that gathereth in summer is a wise son: but he that sleepeth in harvest is a son that causeth shame." The key program, therefore, is the harvest. We are to pray the Lord of THE HARVEST that He will send forth laborers into HIS HARVEST. My friend, the key program of every local church should be the harvest. Churches are not supposed to be social clubs or theological societies or supper clubs. Churches are to be congregations of organized harvesters.

We are to be edified by the teaching of the Word of God that we might evangelize. We are to be blessed by church music in order to stir us to evangelize. Our hearts are to be warmed by Christian fellowship so that we may more effectively and joyfully evangelize. We are to be taught tithing and giving of offerings so that we might more efficiently evangelize. Our entire church format ought to point to the harvest. Our holiness, our happiness and our helpfulness ought all to be tied into the harvest.

Fanny Crosby caught the heartbeat of the harvest when she wrote: "Rescue the perishing, care for the dying, snatch them in pity from sin and the grave; weep o'er the erring one, lift up the fallen, tell them of Jesus the mighty to save. Though they are slighting Him, still He is waiting, waiting the penitent child to receive; plead with them earnestly, plead with them gently, He will forgive if they only believe. Down in the human heart, crushed by the tempter, feelings lie buried that grace can restore; touched by a loving heart, wakened by kindness, chords that are broken will vibrate once more. Rescue the perishing, duty demands it; strength for thy labor the Lord will provide; back to the narrow way patiently win them; tell the poor wanderer a Savior has died." Yes, the harvest is the key program of the church.

The Key People

The key procedure, prayer; the key Person, the Holy Spirit; and the key program, the harvest, are followed by the key people, laborers. Do you recall the perplexing situation stated by Jesus? The harvest is plenteous but the LABORERS are few. Pray therefore the Lord of harvest, "that he will send forth labourers into his harvest." The key people in worldwide evangelization are not celebrities, but LABORERS.

Someone has suggested that the average church is divided into three groups: the shirkers, the jerkers and the workers. The shirkers do nothing; the harvest would be lost if they had to be depended upon to reap. The jerkers are only spasmodic in their interest. The workers are the need of the hour. Not the lazy, not the loafing, but the laborers are the summertime's demand.

"Jesus saith unto them, My meat is to do the will of him that sent me, and to finish his work. Say not ye, There are yet four months, and then cometh harvest? behold, I say unto you, Lift up your eyes, and look on the fields; for they are white already to harvest. And he that reapeth receiveth wages, and gathereth fruit unto life eternal: that both he that soweth and he that reapeth may rejoice together.... other men laboured, and ye are entered into their labours" (John 4:34-38). Will you be a key person in the harvest? The world needs to hear that Christ died for our sins, was buried and rose again the third day. Will you tell them? The message is: Believe on the Lord Jesus Christ and thou shalt be saved. Join us in telling that message to the world.

2

Evangelism

ONE OF the unhealthy trends I have noted over the past decade among fundamental churches is the increasing scarcity of evangelistic campaigns in the local churches. Family seminars, Bible conferences and prophecy conferences can never produce the results of the evangelistic campaign that concentrates on soul-winning, anointed gospel preaching and the mobilized efforts of an entire congregation to reach the lost of the community. As I see it, too many churches have so many programs, clubs and fellowships that they have programmed themselves out of time for evangelism, and clubbed themselves and fellowshiped themselves right out of the ministry of a New Testament church. One pastor told me he has so many board meetings and so many committee meetings to attend, he is "board" to death and "committed" for life! But it really is a serious matter. Gifted itinerant evangelists are finding themselves on the outside looking in as far as many churches are concerned. One pastor who has just assumed the pastorate of his church told me he was shocked to learn the church has not had an evangelistic campaign for the past ten years. Brethren, these things ought not so to be! I do not believe television or radio can take the place of local church evangelistic meetings that are prepared for meticulously, bathed in prayer and well advertised. No electronic medium can replace the eyeball-to-eyeball confrontation of a Spirit-filled evangelist with a sin-sick sinner. The local church that ignores specific times of evangelistic outreach and preaching does so at its own peril.

I believe there is a direct connection between the dwindling number of evangelistic campaigns and the declining Sunday School attendances in fundamental churches over the past ten years. Evangelists tell me their campaigns are seldom Sunday to Sunday anymore. Campaigns have been reduced to Sunday through Friday and in many cases to Sunday through Wednesday. "Weekend revivals" which only cover a Friday through Sunday surely show the sad state of stamina, spirituality and stewardship of American Christians. There is no substitute for extended, extensive, expansive and excited evangelistic meetings with really special music, special attendance efforts and especially special preaching that focuses on the gospel message to sinners. A study of our American church history alone will reveal the great potency of evangelistic campaigns to stir communities, awaken saints and quite dramatically further the work of local churches.

Evangelism Has Improved the Church

Bible-believing Baptist churches have been immeasurably and incalculably blessed by the ministries of true-to-the-Bible evangelists through the years. I can remember well the two-week and three-week campaigns of the 1940s when evangelists like Carl Sweazy and John Carrara stirred my home church, Emmanuel Baptist Church of Toledo, Ohio. Enthusiasm grew with each passing day. Crowds grew each evening. Lives were transformed. Homes were rearranged in a Scriptural response to Scriptural preaching. And the church was healthier for it. Let me name four ways in which evangelistic campaigns have improved the local church down through the centuries.

First, evangelism improved the church because it defined its message. The church must constantly be called back to its glorious task of proclaiming the gospel message. Social reform, ethical renewal, theological education and medical advancement and other noble causes are always in danger of diverting the church from its New Testament responsibility. The apostle Paul wrote: "Moreover, brethren, I declare unto you the gospel which I preached unto you, which also ye have received, and wherein ye stand" (1 Cor. 15:1). Down through the years God-anointed evangelists have said with the apostles: "I declare unto you the gospel." And those evangelists have gone on to define that gospel message just as Paul did in 1 Corinthians 15:3, 4: "For I delivered unto you first of all that which I also received, how that Christ died for our sins according to the scriptures; and that he was buried, and that he rose again the third day according to the scriptures." That pure and simple gospel message needs to be preached with illustrations, integrity and intensity. Our people need devotional preaching, doctrinal preaching and domestic preaching. We need to preach the whole counsel of God. But there needs to be a calling to our pulpits periodically men who are gifted in the earnest effort of proclaiming the evangel. Our congregations must be exposed to messages that rivet the heart and mind and conscience on Calvary, on Christ crucified for sinners. We need to expose our people, who are so prone and tempted to worldliness, to preachers who cry aloud against sin, who make the cross so evidently the answer and who are gifted in "drawing the gospel net."

Evangelists have through the years defined the gospel message in simplicity and power. They have stripped away the sophisticated religious "jargon," the pious sounding platitudes and the crippling churchianity which leaves communities cynical about preachers, contemptible of churches and corrupt in their sins. Too many unchurched people have not the foggiest idea what the church's message is supposed to be. Some perceive it to be a sort of political panacea; others imagine it to be a polite little sermonette on ethics; still others define it as the exposition of some special sectarian dogma that really has no relationship to real people and life as it really is. How we need evangelists who can simply and convincingly define sin, salvation, justification, sanctification and other great gospel themes!

Second, evangelism improved the church because it described its mission. Some churches ought to be called "the First Baptist Cafeteria" or "the Grace Baptist Gymnasium" or "the Calvary Baptist Chorale" or "the Catholic Bingo Parlor." Evangelists have been used by God to call the churches back to the real mission for which they exist. In the eighteenth century mighty men of God like John Wesley, George Whitefield, Jonathan Edwards and others saw churches that had degenerated into social clubs, debating societies and lecture halls. The ecclesiastical leadership had lost its way; the people in the pews were floundering. Who would call with clarion voice the churches back to the Great Commission? The evangelists!

The apostle Paul's words epitomize the focus of the evangelist on the basic mission of the church. He wrote: "For Christ sent me not to baptize, but to preach the gospel: not with wisdom of words, lest the cross of Christ should be made of none effect. For the preaching of the cross is to them that perish foolishness; but unto us which are saved it is the power of God. . . . For I determined not to know anything among you, save Jesus Christ, and him crucified" (1 Cor. 1:17, 18; 2:2). Even some fundamental churches are in danger of getting bogged down with so many programs, one wonders just exactly what their mission in the world is. Have you read your church bulletin lately? Ball games, suppers, canoe trips, miniature golf, etc., etc. How different from the New Testament church that majored on reaching a lost world with the gospel of Christ!

Third, evangelism improved the church because it demonstrated its might. It is true that evangelists do not bring a revival in their satchels, but it is also true that a Spirit-empowered evangelist may be mightily used of God as he preaches the mighty message of the gospel. If anything will awaken a church, thrill a church, excite a church and electrify a church, it is to see sin-hardened teenagers and adults weep their way down church aisles to get saved. The last words of our Lord on earth are recorded in Acts 1:8: "But ye shall receive **power,** after that the Holy [Spirit] is come upon you: and ye shall be witnesses unto me. . . ." Paul wrote: "For I am not ashamed of the gospel of Christ: for it is the **power** of God unto salvation to every one that believeth; to the Jew first, and also to the Greek" (Rom. 1:16). A true church has the most dynamic power in the universe and that power needs to be unleashed. We must not only study the theology of the gospel and the grammar of the gospel and the philosophy of the gospel; we must preach it! We must turn it loose on our communities. We must set aside specific times of concentration on reaching the lost, praying fervently for the conversion of particular sinners. How churches have been blessed by the demonstration of God's power in the transforming of sin-bound men and women! Paul wrote: "And my speech and my preaching was not with enticing words of man's wisdom, but in demonstration of the Spirit and of power: That your faith should not stand in the wisdom of men, but in the power of God" (1 Cor. 2:4, 5).

Fourth, evangelism improved the church because it distinguished its Master. Surely every pastor and every Bible teacher ought to make Christ uppermost in his presentation. Through the years, however, true evangelists have majored on introducing people to the Savior. "And there were certain Greeks among them that came up to worship at the feast: the same came therefore to Philip, which was of Bethsaida of Galilee, and desired him, saying, Sir, we would see Jesus" (John 12:20, 21). **We would see Jesus!** God-anointed evangelists have been used of the Holy Spirit through the centuries to exalt Christ, to center the listener's attention on Him and His finished work. Our churches need more than child psychology or popular "Christian" musical "artists." They need preaching that really and vitally and plainly makes Christ preeminent. HE can save you; HE can heal your marriage; HE can rearrange your home; HE can deliver you from your temper, your lust and yourself. HE said, "And I, if I be lifted up from the earth, will draw all men unto me" (John 12:32). He was lifted up at Calvary. Suspended between Heaven and earth, He died for the sins of mankind. How our churches need evangelistic efforts to magnify that Savior, that mighty Master of the malignant maladies which curse our sin-infested world! Call an evangelist to your church who will cry with faithful fervency: "Behold the Lamb of God, which taketh away the sin of the world."

Evangelism Has Impacted on the Community

Our churches must not become cloistered clubs. Our communities must know who we are and where we are. Our pastors must have "visibility" in their areas. We must become subjects of conversation and objects of genuine interest among the people of our communities. Was that not true of first-century churches? I have stopped at gas stations in small towns and asked for directions to the Baptist church. The man at the pumps, who has lived in town for many years, has often looked at me with a puzzled expression and said, "I don't know where the Baptist church is." Brother, everybody in your town ought to know where your church is. And what better way to make your church known than to plan, advertise and carry out great evangelistic campaigns in your church! Let me list some ways in which evangelists and evangelism have impacted on communities through the years.

First, evangelism impacted upon the community because it redeemed sinners from it. As I write these words my mind goes back through the years to my pastorates where some of the most hardened sinners were saved gloriously as the result of special evangelist efforts. Drunkards, harlots, wife-beaters, drug addicts and proud Pharisees—all were redeemed by the blood of Christ through the preaching of the gospel night after night when God's people were praying earnestly, bringing sinners to the meetings and literally sacrificing other meetings and business appointments and school functions to concentrate on winning the lost.

Let's face it, many churches will not pay the price for successful evangelistic campaigns. A real burden for souls is not there. They will gladly pay forty or fifty dollars to sit nightly through a week of seminars somewhere, but to give themselves to visitation, to the hard work of contacting lost people and bringing them to hear an evangelist is too much. Oh, how we need revival! How we truly need people who are genuinely and sincerely interested in reaching the lost!

Second, evangelism impacted upon the community because it recruited saints for it. Every community needs saintly, godly, spiritual people. Where are we going to get them? Where are we going to get the next generation of Sunday School teachers, the next generation of pastors? Where are we going to get the next generation of deacons and godly church members? **We must get them by winning them.** The pattern was set long ago by Paul himself. "Then came he to Derbe and Lystra: and, behold, a certain disciple was there, named Timotheus, the son of a certain woman, which was a Jewess, and believed; but his father was a Greek: which was well reported of by the brethren that were at Lystra and Iconium. Him would Paul have to go forth with him . . ." (Acts 16:1-3). If Paul is to have a Timothy—if pastors are to have sons in the faith, we must evangelize.

One summer I spoke at our Regular Baptist Camp at Pilot Lake, California. I was thrilled to meet Pastor Howard Kagawa there. Fifteen or sixteen years ago he was a pagan student at Iowa State University. I scheduled an evangelistic campaign to start on a Wednesday night and go through two Sundays, a twelve-day crusade at Campus Baptist Church in Ames. We worked. We prayed. We mobilized. And more than a hundred people walked the aisles during those twelve glorious days. Howard was one of them! He finished at ISU, went on to seminary and is now pastoring a fine church in Sacramento. That campaign with Evangelist Bob Smith, for many years a missionary in Liberia under Baptist Mid-Missions, was used of God to recruit saints for local churches all over America to this day.

Third, evangelism impacted upon the community because it raised standards in it. Isaiah was commanded: "Cry aloud, spare not, lift up thy voice like a trumpet, and show my people their transgression . . ." (Isa. 58:1). What true Christian does not rejoice when he reads of whole cities going "dry" as a result of the mighty preaching of Billy Sunday? Evangelists have always been blessed of God in raising moral standards wherever they have ministered. How many hundreds of places were blessed and uplifted as John R. Rice preached against the scarlet sin, the curse of booze and the blight of secret societies? Oh, people got mad, but Sam Jones, the great southern evangelist, said he would rather people either got mad or got converted than to be passive about the whole thing!

Evangelists have, under God, preached mightily for godliness and righteousness. Dwight L. Moody, William Biederwolf, Billy Sunday, R. A. Torrey, Bob Jones, Sr., in their day, and many faithful evangelists today have proclaimed Biblical standards. Whole families have been revolutionized as dads have quit drinking, moms have quit smoking, teenagers have quit listening to rock music through the Spirit-anointed preaching of a God-called and church-backed evangelist. Make no mistake about it—every church needs to be shaken periodically with the thunder of a prophet's voice. Sins of the flesh and sins of the spirit need to be exposed and dealt with. Biblical standards must be highlighted.

Fourth, evangelism impacted upon the community because it revealed Scriptures to it. The average fundamental Christian has no idea how ignorant the world is of the Bible. The most elementary verses are foreign territory to your unbelieving neighbor. The great Old Testament stories, the New Testament parables and the awesome accounts in the book of Revelation are unknown to the unsaved masses around us. Evangelists have been used of God to open up the Word to the Scripturally ignorant. And how thrilling it is when someone hears John 3:16 for the first time, when the parables of the lost sheep and lost son of Luke 15 are heard for the first time. The great passages of Scripture which have to do with Calvary, the empty tomb, the ascended Lord and the rapture of the Church—all such passages burst upon the sight of the awakening sinner with a drama that is almost breathtaking.

Evangelists are able to introduce people to the Bible, and pastors may then take the converts and teach them, nurture them and disciple them. Pastor, you may be the greatest Bible teacher in your community, but you may need assistance in getting people into your church to discover that you really have something to offer them. I humbly submit to you that an evangelist can be your ally in the battle for truth. Prayerfully plan an evangelistic crusade, mobilize your people to bring in the lost, lead your people to pay for the necessary advertising, pray earnestly for your evangelist and watch God work mightily. The answer to almost any ism or schism is true evangelism.

3

Demonism and Exorcism

When I was pastor at Campus Baptist Church in Ames, Iowa, a national survey indicated that most college and university students and their professors did not believe in the existence of a personal devil. Neither did they believe in the existence of a demon world. The scene now is quite the opposite. Satan-worshiping groups are on the increase. The majority of students today *do* believe in the existence of demons. What has made the difference of opinion in such a short time? One element in the answer is the book by William Peter Blatty, *The Exorcist*. The best-selling book was followed by the box-office-bonanza film, *The Exorcist*. Millions of people read or saw a story of degeneracy, degradation and demonism and exorcism. Another element in the rising interest in the world of demonology is the experience-oriented, doctrine-depleted charismatic movement. Misuse of Scripture, misinterpretation of experience and misrepresentation of the Holy Spirit are tragic traits of today's demonology. We who are fundamental Baptist leaders must know what the New Testament teaches about the work of the Holy Spirit and how His ministry relates to the activity of demons in the lives of human beings. What we teach must not be based on what we think we hear or see or feel but upon what the Word of God says. Many gullible Christians are being shamefully exploited by religious charlatans who are taking advantage of the ignorance of suffering and confused Christians.

The Distinction between Disease and Demonism

If we would be clear on what the New Testament teaches about demonology, we must first note the distinction between disease and demonism. Many people who are supposedly possessed by demons are really the victims of organic disease, psychosomatic disorders or chronic indigestion. To tell these people their problems are demonic is cruel and unchristian. Some highly emotional people who claim to see angels or demons in the middle of the night may only be suffering hallucinations brought on by nervous disorders, drugs, overeating or a combination of all three! Preachers who blame demons for many problems may themselves be suffering from a demon-diagnosis syndrome.

Note a tremendously important distinction highlighted in Matthew 8:16: "When the even was come, they brought unto him many that were possessed with [demons]: and he cast out the spirits with his word, and healed all that were sick." Jesus performed two distinct ministries: He cast out demons and healed the sick. There is a crucial distinction between disease and demonism. **Disease is physical infirmity.** That is a natural phenomenon. **Demonism is spiritual invasion.** That is a supernatural phenomenon. A good physician does not prescribe medicine, treatment or surgery until a proper diagnosis has been made. We who are spiritual physicians dare not do less. To treat a person for demonism when that person is not indeed suffering from demons can be dangerous indeed.

The Difference between Power and Possession

When a person came to me and said, "Pastor, I think I am possessed by a demon," I would ask: "Have you ever received Christ as your personal Savior?" If that person answered, "Yes," I would then ask for a personal testimony. If that individual could give a Scriptural, sincere and assuring testimony of personal faith in Jesus Christ, I would say to that individual, "You do not have a demon. You may be suffering emotionally, physically or financially, but you do not have demons. If you are truly a Christian, you cannot be demon possessed." Now, how could I say that with such assurance? Because there is a vast difference between demon power and demon possession. **Demon power** has to do with the influencing of the mind. **Demon possession** has to do with the indwelling of the body. It is possible for the Christian to be the object of demon power, but **it is impossible for a Christian to be the subject of demon possession.**

Protection from demon possession is provided for us by the Holy Spirit. The indwelling of the Holy Spirit is a guarantee against demon possession. The New Testament makes it clear that every Christian is indwelt by the Holy Spirit at the very moment of personal, saving faith and the reception of Christ as Savior. Romans 8:9: "But ye are not in the flesh, but in the Spirit, if so be that the Spirit of God dwell in you. Now if any man have not the Spirit of Christ, he is none of his." The apostle John, when speaking of the believer's relationship to anti-Christian spirits, writes: "Ye are of God, little children, and have overcome them: because greater is he that is in you, than he that is in the world" (1 John 4:4). The sealing of the Holy Spirit is also a guarantee against demon possession. Ephesians 1:13: "In whom ye also trusted, after that ye heard the word of truth, the gospel of your salvation: in whom also after that ye believed, ye were sealed with that Holy Spirit of promise." Ephesians 4:30: "And grieve not the Holy Spirit of God, whereby ye are sealed unto the day of redemption."

The best illustration of what the New Testament word "seal" means is found in Matthew 27:62-66: "Now the next day, that followed the day of the preparation, the chief priests and Pharisees came together unto Pilate, Saying, Sir, we remember that that deceiver said, while he was yet alive, After three days I will rise again. Command therefore that the sepulchre be made sure until the third day, lest his disciples come by night, and steal him away, and say unto the people, He is risen from the dead: so the last error shall be worse than the first. Pilate said unto them, Ye have a watch: go your way, make it as sure as you can. So they went, and made the sepulchre sure, sealing the stone, and setting a watch." Now the question: Why the seal? To keep Jesus from coming out of the tomb? Of course not! Those Romans did not expect Jesus to walk out of that tomb. They expected the body of Jesus to be stolen by the disciples. The seal was to keep people from breaking into or invading or, if you please, indwelling the interior of that tomb. The seal was to keep the disciples out. The Holy Spirit indwells our bodies and seals them. He Himself is the seal. No demon can invade or indwell the body of a believer in whom dwells the Holy Spirit.

The language of another great New Testament passage demonstrates that our battle against the demon world is not a battle against demon possession but a battle against demon power. Ephesians 6:11-17: "Put on the whole armour of God, that ye may be able to stand against the wiles of the devil. For we wrestle not against flesh and blood, but against principalities, against powers, against the rulers of the darkness of this world, against spiritual wickedness in high places. Wherefore take unto you the whole armour of God, that ye may be able to withstand in the evil day, and having done all, to stand. Stand therefore, having your loins girt about with truth, and having on the breastplate of righteousness; And your feet shod with the preparation of the gospel of peace; Above all, taking the shield of faith, wherewith ye shall be able to quench all the fiery darts of the wicked. And take the helmet of salvation, and the sword of the Spirit, which is the word of God." Armor is to protect against outside, external enemies. The girdle about the loins, the breastplate, the shodding of the feet, the shield, the helmet and the sword are all for the purpose of fighting external foes, not internal ones. If our battle against demonical powers were to be waged against indwelling foes, Paul would have used a much different set of metaphorical analogies.

The fact of the matter is this: We who are Christians cannot be demon-possessed, but we must wage relentless war on the forces of hell outside us. We must be armored upon with truth, righteousness, peace, faith, salvation and the Word of God. Satan cannot indwell us; so his forces bombard us from the outside and through our senses. That is why it is essential to warn our teenagers and adults about the kind of music they listen to, the kind of books they read, the kind of pictures they look upon, the kind of television programs they watch, the kind of companions they spend their time with.

Demons attack our minds even if they cannot abide in our bodies. We must guard against those attacks by employing the panoply of Ephesians 6. The Holy Spirit Who indwells us and seals us against demon possession also empowers us over demon power as we rely upon His resources.

The Diversity between Exposition and Exorcism

What is the responsibility of a New Testament evangelist? What is the responsibility of a New Testament pastor? Is it ever his responsibility to cast out demons? I believe the answer is NO. Our responsibility in this dispensation is the exposition of a message, not the exorcising of demons. Our Lord said: "But ye shall receive power, after that the Holy [Spirit] is come upon you: and YE SHALL BE WITNESSES UNTO ME . . . unto the uttermost part of the earth" (Acts 1:8). Our commission is definitely that of proclaiming a message. But suppose a troubled, shaken, disturbed person comes to my study and says something like the following: "I think I am possessed with a demon. My nights are traumatic with fears and feelings I can't explain. I am thinking wicked and violent thoughts. I sometimes have overpowering urges to commit suicide. It just seems I don't have control over myself." What should I say in response? First, "Are you a Christian?" If the reply is affirmative and convincing, then we must proceed on the assumption the person is **not** demon-possessed. What should I say or do, however, if the person says "I am not a Christian"? Should I walk around my desk, put my hands on that person's head and cry, "Come out, demon, come out in the name of Jesus!"? **I think not.** I should sit down next to that person and show him (or her) Romans 3:23: "For all have sinned, and come short of the glory of God." Then Romans 6:23: "For the wages of sin is death; but the gift of God is eternal life through Jesus Christ our Lord." Then Romans 10:9, 10: "That if thou shalt confess with thy mouth the Lord Jesus, and shalt believe in thine heart that God hath raised him from the dead, thou shalt be saved. For with the heart man believeth unto righteousness; and with the mouth confession is made unto salvation." Then 1 John 5:11, 12: "And this is the record, that God hath given to us eternal life, and this life is in his Son. He that hath the Son hath life; and he that hath not the Son hath not life." If that individual will then bow his head and receive Christ as his Savior, two wonderful things will happen. One, the Holy Spirit will indwell him. Two, if there are demons, they will automatically be exorcised by the Holy Spirit Himself. You see, our responsibility is the exposition of the gospel message. **Exorcism is the ministry of the Holy Spirit.**

It really is a useless exercise to cast demons out of an unsaved person anyhow. If a person is unsaved, he belongs to the devil whether or not he has demons. He is still on his way to hell, demon-possessed or not. Exorcism is as useless as spending one's time trying to get unsaved people to quit smoking or drinking. If you succeed in getting an unsaved person to give up cigarettes, he will simply go to hell smelling better; but he will still go to hell. If you succeed in getting an unsaved person to quit drinking liquor, he will go to hell sober, but he will still go to hell. New Testament preachers are not to be social crusaders or divine healers or demon exorcists. We are to preach the gospel and bring people to a saving knowledge of Christ. A person's greatest need is not to be rid of sickness or freed of demons or removed from a bad environment. A person's greatest need is personal salvation through faith in the shed blood of Christ.

In this day and age Satan has masterfully deceived people, even using passages of Scripture to cleverly confuse them. Just as Satan used Psalm 91:11 and 12 deceitfully when tempting Jesus, so I believe Satan is using Matthew 12:26 to confuse people. Jesus said: "And if Satan cast out Satan, he is divided against himself; how shall then his kingdom stand?" That verse is constantly used by the charismatic exorcisers in defense of their work. But read carefully Matthew 12:43–45: "When the unclean spirit is gone out of a man, he walketh through dry places, seeking rest, and findeth none. Then he saith, I will return into my house from whence I came out; and when he is come, he findeth it empty, swept, and garnished. Then goeth he, and taketh with himself seven other spirits more wicked than himself, and they enter in and dwell there: and the last state of that man is worse than the first." The key word in that passage is *empty*. This is the story of a man who got rid of one demon and ended up with eight! Why? Because he simply got rid of a demon; he was not indwelt by the Holy Spirit. The demon was exorcised, and the man restored himself; "swept, and garnished," to use the language of Scripture. But he was still unsaved. He was still unprotected from further demon possession. Empty!

I am sure Satan would gladly allow one demon to be exorcised temporarily that he might permanently possess such a person with "seven other spirits more wicked." Satan is a deceiver and a cunning destroyer. When you read and hear of unsaved, unchristian people "exorcising demons," you must know, if you are a discerning believer, that something terribly deceitful is taking place. And I fear that Christian charismatic demon-exorcisers are unwittingly playing into the hands of Satan when they supposedly cast out demons. If a person is truly saved, he does not need an exorcist. If an individual is not saved, he still does not need an exorcist, even if he is demon-possessed; he needs a gospel witness.

Matthew 12:26 and Matthew 12:43-45 should be read in the light of Matthew 7:21-23: "Not every one that saith unto me, Lord, Lord, shall enter into the kingdom of heaven; but he that doeth the will of my Father which is in heaven. Many will say to me in that day, Lord, Lord, have we not prophesied in thy name? And in thy name have cast out [demons]? and in thy name done many wonderful works? And then will I profess unto them, I never knew you: depart from me, ye that work iniquity." Satan is not divided against himself when he uses exorcism as a device to deceive. He has actually helped himself! Jesus literally calls the exorcists of Matthew 7 "ye that work iniquity." May God help us who are Regular Baptists to prayerfully, carefully and Scripturally teach our people the truth about the Holy Spirit and also the truth about demonology.

4

The Primacy of Preaching

IN THE December 31, 1979, issue of *Time*, there was a most interesting and provocative article entitled "American Preaching: A Dying Art?" Following are some excerpts from that article:

" 'The Word became flesh,' says John's Gospel of the incarnate Christ of Bethlehem. In Christmas sermons before some 75 million Americans this week, words about Christ will become flesh in the person of the preacher. Through their strange and marvelous craft, Christianity has been transmitted and reshaped for every age since Christ himself went 'preaching the Gospel of the kingdom.' For many American churchgoers, though, a Sunday sermon is something merely to be endured. Many preachers, and parishioners alike, think that passionate and skillful preaching has grown rarer and rarer in individual congregations in the postwar years. The chilling of the Word is a major contributor to the evident malaise in many a large Protestant denomination these days.

"For Roman Catholics, the sermon has not been as important, but rather a kind of spiritual hors d'oeuvre before the Eucharist. Otherwise, as Catholic columnist Rick Casey explains, priests might become mere 'performers' like Protestants, and 'upstage the Eucharist.' In Protestantism, however, the sermon is virtually raised to sacrament. Even if all believers are 'priests,' they still need expert guidance. Said Theologian Karl Barth, 'Through the activity of preaching, God himself speaks.' As a result, lackluster sermons strike at the heart of

Protestant religion. One man tempted to think that American preaching is a dying art is George Plagenz of the *Cleveland Press,* who writes an oft acerbic 'review' of a local church service each week, complete with restaurant-type ratings. Instead of cuisine or ambience, he rates worship service, music, sermon and friendliness, granting up to three stars in each category. In nearly two years, Plagenz, who listened to many pulpit greats a generation ago, has found only two preachers worth three stars. Plagenz blames this in part on the backwash of the 1960s. 'A lot of men went into the ministry for reasons other than preaching. They were interested in social action, so now we're stuck with them.' It seemed only natural that in 1969 *The Pulpit,* venerable sister magazine of the *Christian Century,* renamed itself *Christian Ministry.* . . .

"Many preachers devote far too little time to research, reading and writing in sermon preparation. As a result their poorly constructed, poorly thought-out addresses wander from point to point, and listeners' minds wander too. Lack of effort is not necessarily a sign of sloth. Ministers increasingly are expected to bear heavy loads of counseling and administration that nibble away their time. One rule of thumb is to spend 'an hour in the study for each minute in the pulpit.' But many modern preachers say they are lucky to manage half that. The problems are compounded when the clergyman is a liberal in theology, which may mean that he is uncertain about the importance and accuracy of the Bible or even about the urgent need for biblical teaching. Seminary instruction in homiletics (the techniques of sermon preparation) is generally good. But to conservative critics this work is often undermined by Bible faculties. 'Seminarians are not sure God is speaking in the Bible,' says James Boice of Philadelphia's Tenth Presbyterian Church. 'The professors think of the Bible as a collection of human documents. Centuries ago, even the heretics believed the Bible was the Word of God; they were just wrong in the way they interpreted it. . . .'

"The graduates face a formidable challenge. Churchgoers today are 'theologically illiterate,' says Lutheran Minister Richard John Newhaus in *Freedom for the Ministry.* A lot of things have to be explained rather than taken for granted. (A recent *Christianity Today* Gallup survey showed that while 84% of Americans believe the Ten Commandments are still valid, more than half could not even identify five of them.) Preachers have less time in which to do the explaining, too. Says Donald Macleod, who has taught homiletics at Princeton for 32 years, 'The minds of listeners are geared to TV and the 30-second commercial.' While Macleod insists on an 18-minute maximum, in former times sermons would run more than an hour. Ministers commanded an authority that would be unthinkable today. They could give full play to *docere, delectar, flectere* (to teach, to delight, to move), three purposes of preaching once listed by St. Augustine. The most famous sermon ever preached in America was Jonathan Edwards' 'Sinners in the Hands of an Angry God,' which compared the sinner's plight to 'a spider or loathsome insect' held over a fire. When Edwards preached, all New England shook in its boots. But the so-called Golden Age of Preaching did not come until the 19th century. . . .

"Today the pendulum is swinging back in favor of preaching. When search committees are scouting about for a minister to hire, the top things they are likely to look for are, as an old adage puts it, (1) Preaching. (2) Preaching. (3) Preaching. Right now there are around 200,000 Protestant preachers in America. . . . Like poetry, preaching is always a mystery. Each Sunday brings the danger of failure, and with that the question of potential impact. In his intriguing little book on preaching, *Telling the Truth,* novelist and sometimes preacher Frederick Buechner describes the magic moment when the minister steps into the pulpit. In the pews sit a college student there against his will, a banker who twice contemplated suicide that week, a contractor on the take, a pregnant girl who feels life stir within her, a teacher hiding his homosexuality. 'The preacher pulls the little cord that turns on the lectern light and deals out his note cards like a riverboat gambler. The stakes have never been higher. Two minutes from now he may have lost his listeners completely to their own thoughts, but at this moment he has them in the palm of his hand. The silence in the shabby church is deafening because everybody is listening to it. Everybody is listening including himself. Everybody knows the kind of things he has told them before and not told them, but who knows what this time, out of the silence, he will tell them?'"

What will you tell your congregation? What you tell them may be the determining factor between life and death, a rehabilitated marriage and divorce, heretical confusion and sound doctrine. Surely Biblical preaching is the preeminent need of the 1980s. Read the following "preacher's creed" carefully before we point out some vital characteristics of Biblical preaching. The apostle Paul wrote: "And I, brethren, when I came to you, came not with excellency of speech or of wisdom, declaring unto you the testimony of God. For I determined not to know any thing among you, save Jesus Christ, and him crucified. And I was with you in weakness, and in fear, and in much trembling. And my speech and my preaching was not with enticing words of man's wisdom, but in demonstration of the Spirit and of power: That your faith should not stand in the wisdom of men, but in the power of God" (1 Cor. 2:1-5).

Biblical Preaching Reaches the Emotions

People are hurting. The Greatest Preacher of all declared: "The Spirit of the Lord is upon me, because he hath anointed me to preach the gospel to the poor; he hath sent me to heal the brokenhearted, to preach deliverance to the captives, and recovering of sight to the blind, to set at liberty them that are bruised" (Luke 4:18).

Our congregations, like His, are full of poor, brokenhearted, enslaved, blind, bruised people. Although our preaching must of necessity speak to the intellect and the will, we must also preach to the emotional needs of people. The Word of God has much to say on the subjects of love, hate, fear, lust, depression and willfulness. Great portions of the Psalms, Proverbs and Epistles speak to these crying emotional needs. Preaching must not concern itself with only dry data, sterile statistics and ho-hum history. We must preach truth that touches, faith that feels, doctrine that delights, biography that blesses, gospel that grips. Our expositions must embrace, our sermons must stir, our homilies must heal, our pulpits must pulsate. Jesus preached to hearts when He told of the Prodigal Son, the Good Samaritan and the Rich Man in hell. Jesus spoke of the love of God; He gave answers to troubled hearts. He said, "Fear not, little flock" (Luke 12:32). It is true that we must "afflict the comfortable," but we must also be sure to "comfort the afflicted." If our preaching more effectively reached the emotions of our people, fewer pastors would have to pose as part-time psychologists. We have a message that offers "the peace of God, which passeth all understanding" (Phil. 4:7). Let's preach that peace!

Biblical Preaching Reveals Enthusiasm

Why is it that television actors treat fiction as if it were the faith while preachers too often treat the faith as if it were fiction? Too many pulpits are manned by animated question marks when what those pulpits sorely need are assertive exclamation points. If your message is going to grip your hearer, it must first of all grip you! How can we preachers deal with Heaven and hell issues with such urbane coolness? How can we be so lifeless about eternal life, so deadly boring when we speak of eternity? I am not saying we have to be arm-waving, knee-slapping, hollering pulpit-pounders. But there ought to be a Spirit-engendered fervency and warmth that is apparent to our listeners. They ought to detect in us an enthusiasm for the Lord Jesus Christ. Our love for Him ought to glow in our faces. Surely we ought to be able to talk about the person and work of Christ with genuine enthusiasm! Our congregations ought to sense in us an enthusiasm for the Bible. My text should touch **me;** my message should move **me;** my subject should stir **me.** The Bible should bless **me.** Your people ought to know that you spend time in the Book; you love the Book; you know the Book; you revel in the Word of God! Tape your messages and listen to them. If your delivery is lackluster, if your voice is flat, if your presentation is perfunctory, if you don't sound believable, then do something about it! The stakes are too high to simply maintain mediocrity.

In the Letters to the Editor in *Time* for January 28, 1980, a Presbyterian preacher responded to the article from which we have quoted. He wrote, "I myself employed a speech instructor to work with me on my preaching after noticing that I was bored halfway through the sermon."

Preaching is communication, and we should be conveying to our people an enthusiasm for the Son of God and the Word of God that will be truly contagious.

Biblical Preaching Recognizes Enemies

A pastor is a shepherd. A true shepherd must not only **guide;** he must **guard** his sheep. The apostle Paul set the standard for every New Testament pastor-preacher: "Wherefore I take you to record this day, that I am pure from the blood of all men. For I have not shunned to declare unto you all the counsel of God. Take heed therefore unto yourselves, and to all the flock, over the which the Holy Spirit hath made you overseers, to feed the church of God, which He hath purchased with His own blood. For I know this, that after my departing shall grievous wolves enter in among you, not sparing the flock. Also of your own selves shall men arise, speaking perverse things, to draw away disciples after them. Therefore watch, and remember, that by the space of three years I ceased not to warn every one night and day with tears" (Acts 20:26-31).

This same apostle Paul later told Timothy: "Preach the word; be instant in season, out of season; reprove, rebuke, exhort with all longsuffering and doctrine. For the time will come when they will not endure sound doctrine; but after their own lusts shall they heap to themselves teachers, having itching ears; and they shall turn away their ears from the truth, and shall be turned unto fables. But watch thou in all things, endure afflictions, do the work of an evangelist, make full proof of thy ministry" (2 Tim. 4:2-5).

The gospel has enemies! The Word of God has enemies! The Church has enemies! If we are regular Baptists, it is obviously true that there are irregular Baptists! A faithful pastor-preacher will identify enemies, instruct his people about enemy doctrine and immunize his people against heresy with doses of pure doctrine. Biblical preaching will respond positively to the words of 1 John 4:1: "Beloved, believe not every spirit, but try the spirits whether they are of God: because many false prophets are gone out into the world."

Biblical Preaching Respects Eternity

Fundamentalists have often been accused of being "so heavenly minded that they are no earthly good." We have been told our theology is "pie-in-the-sky platitudes." Such misrepresentations of Biblical ministry and Biblical theology are deliberate distortions of apostolic examples and exhortations. John wrote: "He which testifieth these things saith, Surely I come quickly. Amen. Even so, come, Lord Jesus" (Rev. 22:20). Peter declared: "Nevertheless we, according to His promise, look for new heavens and a new earth, wherein dwelleth righteousness. Wherefore, beloved, seeing that ye look for such things, be diligent that ye may be found of Him in peace, without spot, and blameless" (2 Pet. 3:13, 14). Paul commanded: "Set your affection on things above, not on things on the earth. For ye are dead, and your life is hid with Christ in God. When Christ, Who is our life, shall appear, then shall ye also appear with Him in glory" (Col. 3:2–4).

We, like John, Peter and Paul, must keep our listeners' attention riveted to eternal verities, eternal values and eternal victories. Social gospelers are so earthly minded they are no heavenly good! They are time-wise and eternity-foolish. But we must, like Paul, believe and preach: "For our light affliction, which is but for a moment, worketh for us a far more exceeding and eternal weight of glory; While we look not at the things which are seen, but at the things which are not seen: for the things which are seen are temporal; but the things which are not seen are eternal" (2 Cor. 4:17, 18). We must teach our congregations that they are not really prepared to live until they are prepared to die. They are not genuinely earth-benefactors until they are Heaven-born and Heaven-blessed.

Biblical Preaching Radiates Evangelism

Down through the decades the echo of Richard Baxter's words has haunted every generation of Biblical preachers: "I preached as never sure to preach again, and as a dying man to dying men."

If the people in the pews are ever to have a heartbeat for a lost and dying world, the preachers in the pulpit must radiate evangelistic concern and evangelistic zeal consistently. Do your people know your heart longs to see people saved? Do they sense an urgency about your message? Does your sermon ever sob, your message ever mourn, your preaching ever pulsate, your words ever weep because men are hell-bound, sin-bound and Satan-bound? Oh, that the blood of Christ might drench our discourses! That the tears of Christ might flow over our testimonies! How few of us, if any, can say with Paul: "I say the truth in Christ, I lie not, my conscience also bearing me witness in the Holy [Spirit], That I have great heaviness and continual sorrow in my heart. For I could wish that myself were accursed from Christ for my brethren, my kinsmen according to the flesh" (Rom. 9:1-3).

As we contend for the faith, we must win people to the faith. As we defend our doctrines, we must disciple our converts. Separatists must be soul-winners. Jesus said: "Follow me, and I will make you fishers of men" (Matt. 4:19). If you are truly following Jesus, you will be fishing for men. If you are not fishing, you are not really following.

May God give us a mighty army of preachers who reach the emotions of hurting people, reveal enthusiasm for the Savior and the Scriptures, recognize enemies and expose them, respect eternity and radiate evangelism. Such preaching will incalculably further the health and holiness of our churches.

5

Reincarnation or Resurrection?

REGULAR BAPTISTS are militant fundamentalists in the truest sense. The General Association of Regular Baptist Churches stands without apology or compromise for the fundamentals of the Christian faith as revealed in the infallible, inerrant Word of God, the Bible. Our Biblical position is opposed to religious infidelity in any form. We believe that new evangelicals who make concessions to or compromise with religious infidels for the sake of cooperation in denominational or evangelistic programs are unscriptural. Regular Baptists are also ministering fundamentalists in the best sense. We believe in ministering to the spiritual needs of our people. This means discipleship and indoctrination. We believe in defending the faith against teachings which are contrary to the faith once and for all delivered to the saints. Standing for the fundamentals of the faith means opposing enemy doctrine with clear Biblical truth.

The Bible doctrine of bodily resurrection is under ceaseless and subtle attack today. The influence and impact of oriental religious philosophies are undermining the confidence of masses of humanity in what God's Word says about the future of human beings after death. The doctrine of reincarnation has never been more popular in the western world. Pastors and Christian leaders must be prepared to oppose this theory that strikes at the very heart of our gospel preaching.

Reincarnation is the theory that a person can come back to earth again, after death, in a different form. For example, perhaps George Washington is alive today as a majestic lion. Perhaps some politician today was once on the earth as a Roman Caesar or a French Napoleon. How dangerous is that theory? How important is the Bible doctrine of personal resurrection? Why is it vital to Christianity? I want to answer such questions in this chapter because I believe there are very weighty and conclusive Biblical reasons against the theory of reincarnation. These Biblical arguments support, of course, the Christian doctrine of resurrection for which Paul argued in 1 Corinthians 15:12-19: "Now if Christ be preached that he rose from the dead, how say some among you that there is no resurrection of the dead? But if there be no resurrection of the dead, then is Christ not risen: And if Christ be not risen, then is our preaching vain, and your faith is also vain. Yea, and we are found false witnesses of God; because we have testified of God that he raised up Christ: whom he raised not up, if so be that the dead rise not. For if the dead rise not, then is not Christ raised: And if Christ be not raised, your faith is vain; ye are yet in your sins. Then they also which are fallen asleep in Christ are perished. If in this life only we have hope in Christ, we are of all men most miserable."

The Individuality of Each Person

The Bible teaches clearly the unique individuality of each person. Personal activity has unending consequences. What an individual does in this life has results in the next life for that very same individual. "He that believeth on the Son hath everlasting life: and he that believeth not the Son shall not see life; but the wrath of God abideth on him" (John 3:36). Personal accountability is a certainty. Romans 14:12, "So then every one of us shall give account of himself to God." Reincarnation denies that verse of Scripture. The teaching of reincarnation is a denial of the special reality of every person's works and a denial of the special responsibility of each individual before God. The Bible also teaches the preeminent ascendance of man over all other creatures. Reincarnation can be a kind of evolution in reverse! In this century you may be a man; in the next century you may be a monkey; in the next a frog. Such a teaching is absolutely contrary to the dignity of human individuality. Just as Abraham Lincoln argued for the indivisibility of the union, so the Bible argues for the indivisibility of the individual. We are not in a long, centuries-old process of becoming another person or being. We are individuals and must, for all of eternity, be accountable and responsible for our actions, words and thoughts.

The Immortality of Each Person

Dr. Calvin D. Linton has written: "To millions, the inevitability of individual death demonstrates irrefutably the ultimate absurdity of the universe. That which is inescapably doomed to nothingness can make no valid claim to significance, meaning, or identity. The materialistic existentialist may try to make anxiety itself, the fear of non-being, become the basis of being; and the mystic may try to conceive of nothingness as the ultimate good. But neither can touch the unassuageable yearning of the human consciousness for redemption and continuation, for illumination and fulfillment, for purposeful being and timelessness." Henry T. Buckle declared: "If immortality be untrue, it matters little whether anything else be true or not." Well, praise God for "our Saviour Jesus Christ, who hath abolished death, and hath brought life and immortality to light through the gospel" (2 Tim. 1:10).

Jesus told about two men who illustrate the Biblical teaching on immortality. "There was a certain rich man, which was clothed in purple and fine linen, and fared sumptuously every day: And there was a certain beggar named Lazarus, which was laid at his gate, full of sores, and desiring to be fed with the crumbs which fell from the rich man's table: moreover the dogs came and licked his sores. And it came to pass, that the beggar died, and was carried by the angels into Abraham's bosom: the rich man also died, and was buried; And in hell he lift up his eyes, being in torments, and seeth Abraham afar off, and Lazarus in his bosom. And he cried and said, Father Abraham, have mercy on me, and send Lazarus, that he may dip the tip of his finger in water, and cool my tongue; for I am tormented in this flame. But Abraham said, Son, remember that thou in thy lifetime receivedst thy good things, and likewise Lazarus evil things: but now he is comforted, and thou art tormented" (Luke 16:19–25).

This account shows clearly the immortality of persons and principles. When we say a person is "mortally wounded," we mean that person is going to suffer bodily death. But the real person who lives in that body will go on living, because human beings are immortal souls. You must live forever in Heaven or hell, but live you must. To live forever without God is described in the Bible as eternal death. To live forever with God is defined as eternal life. But both are conscious existences. The human soul is immortal and self-conscious. We do not die like animals. The wicked man described by Jesus went to hell. He did not come back to earth as another human being. Neither did he come back reincarnated as an animal or a bird or an insect. His person is immortal and his destiny is fixed. The same principles are true of the other man, Lazarus, and of you, dear reader. There is no escape from yourself. There is an eternity to be you! In speaking of the eternal and immutable immortality of human souls, Revelation 22:11 reads: "He that is unjust, let him be unjust still; and he which is filthy, let him be filthy still: and he that is righteous, let him be righteous still: and he that is holy, let him be holy still." Unsaved people who die unsaved are unsaved forever. Believers are believers forever. You will be you a million years from now!

One well-known believer in reincarnation is Ann Fisher, a professional psychic consultant and medium who has an office in Albany, New York. Fisher hosts her own TV show and has appeared as a celebrity on a number of radio and TV talks shows around the country. Her viewpoints are being accepted readily on the campuses of secular universities and colleges in America. Her words will serve to show the unbiblical nature of the theory of reincarnation. She declares: "Karma is a Sanskrit word meaning action or reaction or simple cause-and-effect. Christians say, 'As you sow, so shall you reap' or 'do unto others as it should be done unto you!' Most Christians see the cause and effect taking place during one life, whereas Reincarnationists carry it over from one life to another. According to the Law of Karma, a person is born into many lifetimes under the exact set of circumstances with the exact endowment he would need to utilize his best qualities, which he has found and developed in previous lifetimes. There is an appeal to reincarnation that makes it easier for more and more people in the West to accept. The opportunity to meet fresh challenges in new lives is now received by many who would rather believe in rebirth than the old cut-and-dried theory of Heaven or Hell. It appeals to one's sense of fairness. It is a concept of evolution based on the laws of cause and effect. During the time between your last death and your present birth, you have chosen the situation in which you now find yourself, in order to correct past errors. You spin around in the wheels of life. You may sometimes be rich and sometimes poor, changing from time to time in sex and race. Many believers think that every possible type of existence can occur to anyone on earth during their many incarnations" (Quoted in *The Practical Side of Reincarnation,* by David Graham, pp. 152, 153). Surely this teaching is contrary to Biblical immortality.

The Injustices of Reincarnation

First, reincarnation is **unjust to Biblical history.** As an example of what I mean, look at Genesis 25:8: "Then Abraham gave up the ghost, and died in a good old age, an old man, and full of years; and was gathered to his people." Did you get that? He was "gathered to his people." Obviously he could not have been gathered to his people if they were now insects or frogs or monkeys or kangaroos or pigs (perish the thought!) or other people. He could only have been gathered to his people if they were still his people and their souls were where his soul was surely going. Jesus used this historical argument one day when He was talking to the unbelieving Sadducees about the resurrection of the dead. He said: "But as touching the resurrection of the dead, have ye not read that which was spoken unto you by God, saying, I am the God of Abraham, and the God of Isaac, and the God of Jacob? God is not the God of the dead, but of the living" (Matt. 22:31, 32). When Jesus spoke those words, Abraham had been dead for about nineteen hundred years. Isaac and Jacob, likewise, had been dead for many centuries. Then what was Jesus saying? He was simply saying that Abraham, Isaac and Jacob were consciously alive in the very presence of God. Their bodies had turned to dust in Palestinian tombs, but the real Abraham, the real Isaac and the real Jacob were very much alive. The future resurrection will give them glorified and incorruptible bodies, and they will be forever, as they are now, Abraham, Isaac and Jacob, just as you will always be you. Bible Christianity has thus always dignified the eternal worth of the individual just as Old Testament Judaism did. So the theory of reincarnation is an injustice to Biblical history which assures us that Samuel, David and many others "were gathered to their people."

Second, reincarnation is **unjust to Biblical prophecy.** In 1 Thessalonians 4, Paul says: "But I would not have you to be ignorant, brethren, concerning them which are asleep, that ye sorrow not, even as others which have no hope. For if we believe that Jesus died and rose again, even so them also which sleep in Jesus will God bring with him. . . . and the dead in Christ shall rise first: . . . Wherefore comfort one another with these words" (1 Thess. 4:13-18). Wherein was the comfort for those Thessalonian Christians? Just this—they could be sure their dead loved ones would someday be raised from the dead. They would be recognizable, because they would be the same people they had buried! Reincarnation had not robbed them of their immortal identification and unique personalities. Bible prophecy about bodily resurrection and reunion would be a farce if the theory of reincarnation were true. No Christian comfort would be possible.

Third, reincarnation is **unjust to Biblical salvation.** Dr. Rene Pache has written: "The whole theory of reincarnations is based on the pagan notion of the slow amelioration of man by his own efforts and of the expiatory value of his sufferings. From one existence to another, man purifies himself so as to save himself. But the utter absurdity is that he has no memory of his past lives; thus, he suffers without knowing why. Moreover, if he wants to behave ignobly, he is always under the delusion that he will be able to make up for such behavior in a future life. For some, man can be reborn only as a man; for others, he appears under the form of all kinds of animals. That almost infinite repetition of reincarnations (six hundred thousand times, they say in India) becomes so exhausting and desperate that man's principal concern is to be liberated from it: salvation is the nirvana, or the absence of desire and sensation and thus the end of suffering, an abandonment to the great whole. It is difficult to find a more ridiculous doctrine, one more inimical to life and more contrary to all the teachings of the Bible. The favor that it enjoys, along with its entire procession of Hindu doctrines and practices, is a proof of the apostasy of our formerly 'christianized' world" (*The Future Life*, pp. 92, 93, published by Moody Press; this book of 376 pages is well worth your money).

Study carefully the last two verses of the ninth chapter of Hebrews: "And as it is appointed unto men once to die, but after this the judgment: So Christ was once offered to bear the sins of many; and unto them that look for him shall he appear the second time without sin unto salvation." Salvation from sin, you see, was purchased by the shed blood of the individual Son of God. He died for real people—real, accountable, responsible, immortal, eternal, immutable people. Those who are saved have personally placed their faith in Christ's finished work of redemption. Christ died, was buried and rose from the dead. His death paid the sinner's penalty. His resurrection guarantees the believer's resurrection. Resurrection, not reincarnation, is the hope of the believer in Christ. Paul asked, "Why should it be thought a thing incredible with you, that God should raise the dead?" (Acts 26:8). With this striking question the apostle Paul began his defense before King Agrippa. Let us as Regular Baptists militantly defend the Biblical doctrine of resurrection. Let us militantly preach and teach the fundamental truths of 1 Corinthians 15.

In closing, let me suggest some helpful books for your personal study. *Great Sermons on the Resurrection*, published by Baker Book House, has long been one of my favorite books. It contains eight great messages: "The Living Dead" and "Witnesses of the Resurrection" by Alexander MacLaren; "Death and Resurrection" and "The Resurrection Credible" by C. H. Spurgeon; "The Resurrection of Jesus Christ" and "The Fifteenth Chapter of First Corinthians" by D. L. Moody; "The General Resurrection" by T. DeWitt Talmage; and "Christianity without the Resurrection" by Canon Liddon. This book will fortify your faith and enflame your preaching heart!

If you would like to acquaint yourself with what modern teachers of reincarnation are saying, listed below are some titles. I would **not** recommend your spending your hard-earned money to buy these books. I didn't! Use your local public library. That's what I did! *Born Again: The Truth about Reincarnation,* by Hans Holzer, Doubleday and Company, 267 pages; *Twenty Cases Suggestive of Reincarnation,* by Ian Stevenson of the University of Virginia; *Reincarnation: An East-West Anthology,* The Theosophical Publishing House, 341 pages; *The Practical Side of Reincarnation,* by David Graham, Prentice-Hall, 210 pages; *Many Lifetimes,* by Joan Grant and Dennis Kelsey.

6

Pastoral Perils

PASTORS ARE special people. They have special challenges and opportunities. They are privileged men. Called to teach and preach, they are God's gifts to local churches. They are also men with special perils. As I travel the country, ministering in scores of churches, speaking in conferences to hundreds of pastors and consulting with many of them, I have been made uniquely aware of the dangers deviously lurking along the ministerial highways of service. Pastors are imperiled men! Paul's pastoral epistles abound in references to those perils. He himself was an imperiled man. He said he was "in perils of waters, in perils of robbers, in perils by mine own countrymen, in perils by the heathen, in perils in the city, in perils in the wilderness, in perils in the sea, in perils among false brethren" (2 Cor. 11:26). Perils! My observations of pastors through the years have alerted my thinking to the necessity of constant vigilance "lest that by any means, when I have preached to others, I myself should be a castaway" (1 Cor. 9:27). In this chapter I would like to call attention to what I consider to be the seven most deadly perils dogging the paths of pastors. My prayer is that God will use these words of warning to forearm shepherds who may have been lulled into a false sense of security. For those who are already "watching and praying," these words go forth to further strengthen your holy resolves. Whether we are old or young, experienced or inexperienced, we must recall often the words of Paul: "Wherefore let him that thinketh he standeth take heed lest he fall" (1 Cor. 10:12).

I am going to list these perils in alphabetical order, since it is not really possible to rank them in order of importance or imminent danger. What is a persistent peril to one man may not even bother someone else, but all of the following seven are real dangers. Preachers through the centuries have fallen prey to them, and no wise man of God should consider himself to be immune to any one of these seven pernicious perils.

The Peril of Fame

Probably no Regular Baptist pastor is in any danger of having his picture on the cover of *Time* magazine, but the desire to be popular is a very real peril. Success has produced many failures! Talented men who become accustomed to accomplishment and attainment must be careful to constantly clip the wings of pride. "When pride cometh, then cometh shame" (Prov. 11:2). The Bible is replete with examples of men who fell victim to their own successes and popularity. The names of Saul, Absalom, Uzziah, Peter, Demas and Diotrephes remind us that we can be easily victimized by our own exalted opinions of ourselves. We must persistently remind ourselves that "we preach not ourselves, but Christ Jesus the Lord; and ourselves your servants for Jesus' sake" (2 Cor. 4:5). Like John the Baptist, our attitude must be: "He must increase, but I must decrease" (John 3:30).

There is entirely too much ministerial boasting in the circles of fundamentalism today. Bragging about being bigger, better, faster, richer, higher, deeper, stricter, etc., etc., is foreign to the New Testament attitude. Paul wrote: "For we dare not make ourselves of the number, or compare ourselves with some that commend themselves: but they measuring themselves by themselves, and comparing themselves among themselves, are not wise" (2 Cor. 10:12). "Nay, much more those members of the body, which seem to be more feeble, are necessary: And those members of the body, which we think to be less honourable, upon these we bestow more abundant honour; and our uncomely parts have more abundant comeliness. For our comely parts have no need: but God hath tempered the body together, having given more abundant honour to that part which lacked: That there should be no schism [pronounced sizzim!] in the body, but that the members should have the same care one for another" (1 Cor. 12:22-25). If God blesses your labors with unusual success, remember to give Him the glory. If your church becomes bigger and better than others in your area, humbly thank God for using you. But let us all meditate on the exhortations in Jeremiah and 1 Corinthians: "And seekest thou great things for thyself? seek them not" (Jer. 45:5). "Moreover it is required in stewards, that a man be found faithful. But with me it is a very small thing that I should be judged of you, or of man's judgment . . . but he that judgeth me is the Lord" (1 Cor. 4:2-4).

The Peril of Fear

Many times throughout the Bible we find the exhortation, "fear not." Certainly every Bible-believing preacher ought to be able to adopt Psalm 27:1 as his own personal testimony: "The LORD is my light and my salvation; whom shall I fear? the LORD is the strength of my life; of whom shall I be afraid?" Many pastors have been paralyzed by fear. It is surely true in the pastoral ministry that "the fear of man bringeth a snare" (Prov. 29:25). Some men fear their wives, some fear their children, some are afraid of their deacons, some fear their trustees and some fear "what people will say." How sad! Fear is a peril that perplexes, procrastinates and perverts. The only cure for fearing man is truly fearing God. Joseph said, "I fear God" (Gen. 42:18); so he did not fear his brothers, he did not fear Potiphar's wife, he did not fear Potiphar, and he did not fear Pharaoh. I have sensed a common characteristic possessed by pastors who are genuinely being used of God: the characteristic is fearlessness. To fear no one but God is so vital to the man of God. Paul said to Timothy: "For God hath not given us the spirit of fear; but of power, and of love, and of a sound mind. Be not thou therefore ashamed of the testimony of our Lord, nor of me his prisoner: but be thou partaker of the affictions of the gospel according to the power of God" (2 Tim. 1:7, 8).

We often refer to the Baptist pastor as "the undershepherd." But some church members and pastors have evidently taken the term to mean something demeaning. Pastors are called undershepherds, not because they are "under" the board of deacons or "under" the board of trustees but because they are under the Chief Shepherd. It is true that pastors are not to be dictators, but neither are they to be dictated to! They are not to be lords, but neither are they to be lackeys. In fact, the Bible refers to **under**shepherds as **over**seers (Acts 20:28). Our churches desperately need pastors who exercise pastoral authority lovingly but firmly, learnedly but fearlessly, longsufferingly but faithfully. The fearless man of God must teach his people Hebrews 13:17: "Obey them that have the rule over you, and submit yourselves: for they watch for your souls, as they that must give account, that they may do it with joy, and not with grief: for that is unprofitable for you."

The Peril of Feasting

I thought about heading this section the peril of fat or the peril of flab! Many of our preachers have pirate's disease—sunken chests! Others have the furniture affliction—their chests have dropped into their drawers! Seriously, though, there is real and crippling peril involved in our physically sedentary way of life characterized by overeating and underexercising. It is a shame to see so many pastors incapacitated by hypertension, heart disease and other illnesses brought on by poor health habits. American males are famous the world over for digging their graves with their forks. Many preachers die prematurely because they failed to treat their bodies as sacred temples of the Holy Spirit. Gluttony and physical laziness are enemies to godliness and spiritual life.

We do rightly to counsel against cigarette smoking, drug use, the drinking of alcoholic beverages and sexual promiscuity on the basis of 1 Corinthians 6:19, 20: "What? know ye not that your body is the temple of the Holy [Spirit] which is in you, which ye have of God, and ye are not your own? For ye are bought with a price: therefore glorify God in your body, and in your spirit, which are God's." But let's also apply that passage to overselves. The preacher's body is important. How many men are there whose ambition to make pastoral calls, whose ability to study effectively for long periods of time, whose attitudes toward people and life in general are substandard because of excessive weight and lack of physical exercise? I do not advocate your buying expensive athletic equipment or suddenly deciding you are going to be a jogger or racquet-ball fanatic. But you can walk briskly for twenty or thirty minutes a day. Do you say you can't afford to take the time? My friend, you can't afford not to take the time! We must take time for our devotional life. And we must make time to keep our physical hearts in good condition. The twin perils, eating and lack of exercise, really plague many men of God. Food becomes a foe. Comfort becomes a combatant. Ease becomes an enemy. An interesting verse at this point is Ecclesiastes 10:17: "Blessed art thou, O land, when thy king is the son of nobles, and thy princes [how about pastors?] eat in due season, for strength, and not for drunkenness!" Another good bit of ancient advice is in Proverbs 23:1, 2: "When thou sittest to eat with a ruler, consider diligently what is before thee: And put a knife to thy throat, if thou be a man given to appetite." Discipleship has to do with real, practical discipline in every area of life. Paul wrote: "And every man that striveth for the mastery is temperate in all things . . . I keep under my body, and bring it into subjection" (1 Cor. 9:25, 27). Being careful to spend more time in the "upper room" and less time in the "supper room" might be of great benefit to both body and spirit. To be sure, holiness and healthiness need not be mutually exclusive.

The Peril of Finances

It is noteworthy that Paul warned Timothy very pointedly about the danger of money. One of the qualifications for pastors is "not greedy of filthy lucre" (1 Tim. 3:3). The desire for dollars can be dangerous. "But they that will be rich fall into temptation and a snare, and into many foolish and hurtful lusts, which drown men in destruction and perdition. For the love of money is the root of all evil: which while some coveted after, they have erred from the faith, and pierced themselves through with many sorrows. But thou, O man of God, flee these things" (1 Tim. 6:9–11). Our Lord said, "Ye cannot serve God and [money]" (Matt. 6:24). He also declared: "Take heed, and beware of covetousness: for a man's life consisteth not in the abundance of the things which he possesseth" (Luke 12:15).

Many a preacher has ruined his testimony in his community by not paying his bills. We must beware of the credit card mania and the constant enticement to live beyond our means. Pastors should be tithers, savers and budgetmakers. Talking frankly to trustees about hospitalization, life insurance, housing needs and driving expenses is the responsibility of a pastor. Stewardship must be taught by the pastor as faithfully as he teaches other matters of doctrine and decorum. Finances and faith need not be enemies. Paul's epistles abound with references to wise and practical stewardship. Churches must be taught how to care for pastors. And pastors must be honest in all of their financial dealings. Paul also told Timothy that a pastor is to be "given to hospitality" (1 Tim. 3:2). If our dollars are dedicated to Christ, if our silver is sanctifed to His glory, money will be our servant, not our sovereign.

The Peril of Flirting

The number of preachers who fall into sexual immorality is, frankly, disheartening. When I was studying for the ministry thirty years ago, I often heard that preachers face three grave dangers, fame, finances and females. Another teacher of preachers warned "Beware of the headlines and the hemlines." Still another preached: "Solomon was the victim of lucre and lust." Always in the warnings somewhere women were involved. As I move around America in my work as National Representative, I now know why the warnings were so insistent and persistent. The peril is seemingly omnipresent and surely ominous. The tragedy of broken ministries, broken hearts and broken homes is sickening. And it all usually begins with wandering eyes, careless hands and flirtatious words. How careful preachers ought to be in their relationships with the opposite sex! Let me give some suggestions which may help.

First, pastors ought to maintain a "hands-off" policy toward women. Long, lingering handshakes, putting your arm around a woman's waist or shoulders should be "no-nos." Call me prudish if you will, but sometimes "innocent contact" can result in "incinerating concords." "Can a man take fire in his bosom, and his clothes not be burned? Can one go upon hot coals, and his feet not be burned? So he that goeth in to his neighbour's wife; whosoever toucheth her shall not be innocent" (Prov. 6:27-29). Second, do not counsel with a woman alone. It is good practice to require a woman's husband to be present, or if that is not feasible, your own wife should be there. If you are counseling an unmarried woman, your wife or secretary ought to be close to the study door, if not in the room with you. I would rather be too careful than too careless. Third, do not call on a woman when that woman is alone in her residence. Take your wife with you. Fourth, guard your thought life. Paul told Timothy to flee youthful lusts (2 Tim. 2:22). He also advises us to think on things that are true, honest, just, pure, lovely and of good report (Phil. 4:8). "Keep thy heart with all diligence; for out of it are the issues of life" (Prov. 4:23). **Desires often become deeds.** Jesus said: ". . . whosoever looketh on a woman to lust after her hath committed adultery with her already in his heart" (Matt. 5:28). Fifth, stay romantically involved with your wife. The Word of God commands: "Let thy fountain be blessed: and rejoice with the wife of thy youth. Let her be as the loving hind and pleasant roe; let her breasts satisfy thee at all times, and be thou ravished always with her love" (Prov. 5:18, 19). Talk to her. Tell her your needs. Be concerned about hers. Buy her things that only husbands buy for wives. Date her. Get a babysitter to watch the children, and take her out regularly, even if you can only afford Wendy's or McDonald's or the Ponderosa! And make sure you always treat her with affection, courtesy and dignity when in the presence of the members of your congregation. Make sure they know your heart belongs to her. In short, love her (Eph. 5:25).

The Peril of Formalism

By formalism I do not mean orderliness. Neither do I mean a well-planned service. I am not opposed to a church bulletin that contains an "order of service." By formalism I mean a dry, cold, unfeeling professionalism which is described by Paul as "having a form of godliness, but denying the power thereof" (2 Tim. 3:5). The pastor must not allow himself to become a heartless technician who treats people like robots and churches like computers. After more than twenty-five years in the ministry, I have conducted scores of weddings, probably hundreds of funerals; I have presided over the Lord's Table hundreds of times. In my last pastorate I baptized more than 420 people. The peril in all of that is that I am so familiar with the procedures, so accustomed to the words and so well-acquainted with the emotions involved that I become desensitized to the realities which are so vital and valid in every one of those services. I must never lose the Spirit-endowed capacity to weep with those who weep, rejoice with those who rejoice, worship with those who worship. To simply mouth phrases with no compassion and no personal identification is horrendous sin. The pastoral prayer, the making of announcements, the reading of Scripture, the preaching of a sermon, the giving of an invitation, the saying of a benediction can all become so perfunctory, so mechanical that minds are unreached, hearts are untouched and lives are unchanged. Dead orthodoxy is the end result of such hideous and unholy formalism. Young people grow up under such professionalism thinking the pastoral ministry to be an act. Adults become mesmerized by a sterile ritualism that leaves them unmoved and uncaring. Attendance becomes a mere habit and worship a comatose charade. How we need to say with the apostle Paul: "And my speech and my preaching was not with enticing words of man's wisdom, but in demonstration of the Spirit and of power: That your faith should not stand in the wisdom of men, **but in the power of God**" (1 Cor. 2:4, 5).

The Peril of Fury

One of the most difficult commands in the Bible is Ephesians 4:26: "Be ye angry, and sin not: let not the sun go down upon your wrath." One of the real perils of the ministry is uncontrolled tempers. It is more than passingly interesting that God has made provision for that need. The fruit of the Spirit includes "temperance" or self-control (Gal. 5:23). Losing one's temper in a congregational business meeting can be a disaster. "Blowing up" at a board meeting can be a spiritual catastrophe. It has been rightly said that long pastorates are not the result of preachers with short fuses. The fruit of the Spirit also inclues longsuffering, gentleness and meekness. Losing his temper kept Moses from entering the Promised Land, and pastoral losses of temper have prevented many otherwise capable men of God from entering a "promised land" of pulpit power and pastoral productivity. "A soft answer turneth away wrath: but grievous words stir up anger" (Prov. 15:1). "He that is soon angry dealeth foolishly" (Prov. 14:17). "He that is slow to anger is better than the mighty; and he that ruleth his spirit than he that taketh a city" (Prov. 16:32). These passages point up the crucial significance of self-control. Many times there is a fine distinction between "righteous indignation" and "being plain mad." The pressures of the ministry, the stress of financial needs and the cantankerous ways of some board members may make your job difficult, preacher friend, but dependence upon God's resources will be far better than "blowing off steam." We in the ministry must make sure we do not take out our frustrations on wife or children. Don't turn the parsonage into a "gripe tank." Peter wrote: "Casting all your care upon Him; for He careth for you" (1 Pet. 5:7). The psalmist counseled: "Cease from anger, and forsake wrath: fret not thyself in any wise to do evil" (Ps. 37:8).

7

Biblical Separation

ACCORDING TO Article II, Section 1, of the GARBC Constitution, an integral part of the purpose for our very existence is "to raise a standard of Biblical separation from worldliness, modernism and apostasy; to emphasize the Biblical teaching that a breakdown of the divinely established lines between Bible believers and apostates is unscriptural and to be a voice repudiating cooperation with movements which attempt to unite true Bible believers and apostates in evangelistic and other cooperative spiritual efforts." We must remain true to that separatist position. We must clearly understand and determine to uphold that sacred Scriptural purpose.

The GARBC is a uniquely separatist Fellowship of churches. Our pastors should be known as separatists. Our approved colleges and seminaries should be known as separatist institutions. The presidents and professors should be known as separatists. Our approved missionary agencies should be known as separatist missionary agencies. Their presidents and their multiplied hundreds of missionaries should be known as separatists. The same goes for our approved social agencies. When people think of Regular Baptists, they ought to think of fundamentalists who are separatists. Our country, and the world, needs an uncompromising, evangelistic, ecclesiastically pure Association of sovereign, Bible-believing, Christ-honoring Baptist churches more than ever. May we not fail to be true to the God of our fathers as we carry the separatist banner. As you take inventory, consider the following.

Biblical Separation Involves Our Attitudes

Biblical separation has to do with an attitude of holiness. Throughout the Word of God, saints of all ages have been admonished to set themselves apart from an ungodly world while at the same time setting themselves apart unto God. The doctrine of Biblical sanctification includes our Biblical practice of separation from that which is unholy and displeasing to God. The Bible warns, in both the Old and New Testaments, against an attitude of friendliness toward and accommodation to the world. In His high priestly prayer, our Savior said: "I have given them thy word; and the world hath hated them, because they are not of the world, even as I am not of the world. I pray not that thou shouldest take them out of the world, but that thou shouldest keep them from the evil. They are not of the world, even as I am not of the world. Sanctify them through thy truth; thy word is truth" (John 17:14-17). The attitude of a believer ought to be, therefore, "otherworldly." A first-century Christian leader who failed to have this attitude became a casualty, and Paul indelibly writes the reason in 2 Timothy 4:10: "For Demas hath forsaken me, having loved this present world." Both personal separation from worldliness and ecclesiastical separation from compromise and apostasy depend on an attitude of loyalty to the God of the Word and the Word of God.

Throughout Scripture this attitude is impressed upon us. "And the LORD spake unto Moses, saying, Speak unto all the congregation of the children of Israel, and say unto them, Ye shall be holy: for I the LORD your God am holy" (Lev. 19:1, 2). "And ye shall not walk in the manners of the nations, which I cast out before you: for they committed all these things, and therefore I abhorred them. . . . I am the LORD your God, which have separated you from other people. . . . And ye shall be holy unto me: for I the LORD am holy, and have severed you from other people, that ye should be mine" (Lev. 20:23-26). Peter's attitude is beautifully translated in the New International Version: "Dear friends, I urge you, as foreigners and strangers in the world, to abstain from sinful desires, which war against your soul. Live such good lives among the pagans that, though they accuse you of doing wrong, they may see your good deeds and glorify God on the day He visits us" (1 Pet. 2:11, 12). That should be our holy attitude: We are aliens and strangers. As the songwriter said: "This world is not my home, I'm just a passing thru." The world's religions, the world's music, the world's life-styles are all foreign to the child of God. The National and World Councils of Churches have not been characterized by that Biblical attitude. The National Association of Evangelicals, in its willingness to cooperate with and compromise with those Councils, has not shown that attitude. Ecumenical evangelism has become entertainment-oriented, new evangelical churches have become worldly and their ecclesiastical machinery has been characterized by a methodology that is absolutely contrary to the attitude expressed by Paul: "For the weapons of our warfare are not carnal, but mighty through God to the pulling down of strong holds" (2 Cor. 10:4).

Biblical Separation Involves Our Associations

In 1932 some courageous men of conviction decided they could no longer be associated with the infidelity in the then Northern Baptist Convention. The separation of these men and their local churches from the Convention was in explicit obedience to the Word of God: "Be ye not unequally yoked together with unbelievers: for what fellowship hath righteousness with unrighteousness? and what communion hath light with darkness? And what concord hath Christ with Belial? or what part hath he that believeth with an infidel? And what agreement hath the temple of God with idols? for ye are the temple of the living God. . . . Wherefore come out from among them, and be ye separate, saith the Lord, and touch not the unclean thing" (2 Cor. 6:14–17). The prophet of old asked: "Can two walk together, except they be agreed?" (Amos 3:3). The obvious answer is no.

The GARBC has insisted upon fidelity to the Word of God on the matter of associations. Our Constitution makes it clear: "Any Baptist church on the North American continent, the United States, and her territorial possessions which is *not* in fellowship or cooperation with any local, state or national convention, association or group which permits the presence of liberals, liberalism (modernists or apostates), and which church subscribes to the Constitution and Articles of Faith" may be considered for fellowship with us. Because we believe Biblical separation demands only Scriptural associations, we have remained separated from the Baptist World Alliance whose membership includes the American Baptist Church, the Baptist General Conference, the Baptist Federation of Canada and the Russian Baptist Church (Communist controlled).

Biblical Separation Involves Our Ambitions

"Then there arose a reasoning among them, which of them should be greatest" (Luke 9:46). Human ambition is a tricky and deceptive motivator. Even those in Christian service can be deceived by the strong desire to "be greatest." If men like Peter, James and John were not immune to the vagaries of ambition, we surely must be on guard against its deceptive devices. Much of the compromise we have seen in the evangelical world during the past half-century has stemmed from a professed ambition to "preach the gospel to the most people possible in the shortest time possible." Years ago Billy Graham said he would go anywhere under any sponsorship in order to preach his message. Such an ambition seems on first sight to be a noble one. But is it?

Ecumenical evangelistic movements have always justified their compromises by their stated ambition to "win souls." In June of 1980, for example, men and women from around the world convened for the Consultation on World Evangelization in Pattaya, Thailand. In the name of "evangelism," charismatic confusion, doctrinal infidelity and ecclesiastical excesses were overlooked. We as Regular Baptists do not discount the importance of evangelism, but we do say that the end does not justify the means. Winning souls is no excuse for disobeying God's clear commands instructing us to separate from unbelief. "Shall we continue in sin, that grace may abound? God forbid" (Rom. 6:1, 2). Our ambitions to have big crowds or large Sunday Schools or great successes must never entice us away from **our primary ambition to obediently do the will of God.**

Biblical Separation Involves Our Affirmations

One of the most difficult problems in dealing with new evangelical non-separatists is their ability to say good things! People will say things like: "But Billy Graham does preach the gospel." "What's wrong with what Oral Roberts says?" "Doesn't Robert Schuller say such helpful things?" However, what non-separatists do not say is also important! Regular Baptists say things that new evangelicals do not say. We do not trim our message to suit our audience. Every separatist ought to be able to say: "For I have not shunned to declare unto you all the counsel of God" (Acts 20:27). Years ago, Dr. David Nettleton wrote a GARBC Literature Item in which he rightfully said the choice is between a limited message or a limited fellowship. We in the GARBC have opted for an unlimited message and a limited fellowship. We have decided to declare the whole counsel of God instead of the "irreducible minimum." We do not believe the Bible is confined to "four spiritual laws." We do not believe that our preaching must be limited to a "positive gospel." We believe in affirming our Baptist distinctives with clarity and conviction.

More than twenty years ago, Dr. Robert T. Ketcham wrote: "It is insisted that Dr. Graham preaches the Gospel in his crusades. This I do not deny, but I am ready to prove that when Dr. Graham is alone with the modernistic crowd, he has an increasing tendency to accommodate his terms to their position. Some years ago he spoke in Union Seminary in New York. I have the tape of his address. I notice on several occasions during that address that he used terminologies which he would never have used had he been speaking before a fundamentalist group. As an illustration of this, whenever he came in his message where the easy, ordinary term for him to use was 'born again' he used the term 'getting men over the line into the kingdom.' This term, of course, exactly suited his audience." Concerning the imperative importance of clear-cut affirmations, Paul wrote: "Now the Spirit speaketh expressly, that in the latter times some shall depart from the faith, giving heed to seducing spirits, and doctrines of devils. . . . If thou put the brethren in remembrance of these things, thou shalt be a good minister of Jesus Christ, nourished up in the words of faith and of good doctrine" (1 Tim. 4:1-6). Regular Baptists are determined to be good ministers!

Biblical Separation Involves Our Affections

The Old Testament tells of believing Jehoshaphat's aliance with ungodly Ahab. A faithful prophet confronted Jehoshaphat and asked: "Shouldest thou help the ungodly, and love them that hate the LORD? therefore is wrath upon thee from before the LORD" (2 Chron. 19:2). There is an inordinate and, of course, an unscriptural emphasis on "love" in Christendom today. Liberals and compromisers are excused for their disobedience to God's Word by the insipid exclamation: "But they are such gracious and loving men!" The apostle Paul was not led astray by such deception. He wrote of infidels in sheep's clothing: "For such are false apostles, deceitful workers, transforming themselves into the apostles of Christ. And no marvel; for Satan himself is transformed into an angel of light. Therefore it is no great thing if his ministers also be transformed as the ministers of righteousness" (2 Cor. 11:13-15). Judas Iscariot is not the only one who has betrayed Christ with a kiss.

Biblical separation demands that we exercise some holy hatred! "Hate the evil, and love the good, and establish judgment in the gate" (Amos 5:15). A gardener who loves flowers must hate weeds. "Love not the world, neither the things that are in the world. If any man love the world, the love of the Father is not in him" (1 John 2:15). Our Lord said to the church at Ephesus: "But this thou hast, that thou hatest the deeds of the Nicolaitanes, which I also hate" (Rev. 2:6). "So hast thou also them that hold the doctrine of the Nicolaitanes, which thing I hate" (Rev. 2:15). Oh, that we might hate the devious deeds and deceitful doctrines of apostate denominations as our Savior does! Oh, that we might cry out with holy hatred against the sanctimonious sins of religious infidels whose damnable doctrines doom their followers to eternal darkness. Love that is born of God truly hates that which is in opposition to God. "Keep yourselves in the love of God, looking for the mercy of our Lord Jesus Christ unto eternal life. And of some have compassion, making a difference: And others save with fear, pulling them out of the fire; hating even the garment spotted by the flesh!" (Jude 21-23).

Biblical Separation Involves Our Activities

As we take inventory of ourselves, we need to meditate long on the great Biblical passages which have always meant so much to separatists: "Look to yourselves, that we lose not those things which we have wrought, but that we receive a full reward. Whosoever transgresseth, and abideth not in the doctrine of Christ, hath not God. He that abideth in the doctrine of Christ, he hath both the Father and the Son. If there come any unto you, and bring not this doctrine, receive him not into your house, neither bid him God speed: For he that biddeth him God speed is partaker of his evil deeds" (2 John 8-11). This passage describes for us some of the regular activities of a truly separatist ministry. First, **we must recognize** false teachers for what they are: transgressors ("whosoever transgresseth"), unbelievers ("abideth not in the doctrine"), ungodly ("hath not God"). Second, **we must rebuke them** for what they believe. Third, **we must relate to them** the truth. Fourth, **we must receive them not.** If the prohibitions are ignored, we become partakers of their evil deeds. Encouraging words to an apostate result in evil works. Untold harm has been done by inclusive evangelism which welcomes the participation of liberals in outreach programs. How we need to pray that believing pastors in the Southern Baptist Convention and American Baptist Church (formerly called Northern Baptist Convention) will see the need to separate from organizations that support colleges and seminaries where the fundamentals of the faith are resisted, ridiculed and rejected! Scriptural activity is not infiltration of such institutions but separation from them.

Biblical Separation Involves Our Academics

Scholarship is not synonymous with spirituality. In fact, colleges and seminaries have all too often been the ruination of once great denominations. Scholarship without spirituality becomes skepticism. "Knowledge puffeth up, but [love buildeth up]. And if any man think that he knoweth anything, he knoweth nothing yet as he ought to know" (1 Cor. 8:1, 2).

Scholarship without the Scriptures precludes spirituality. All, and I mean all, academic pursuits must bow to the authority of the Word of God. If our GARBC movement is to remain virile, vigorous and valid, we must approve only colleges and seminaries that are unashamedly and unabashedly and unwaveringly separatist. Our approved schools must teach Biblical separation from the chapel platform, feature Biblical separatists from their Bible conference platforms and refuse to give a platform to speakers who are not sympathetic to our Biblical and Associational position.

Paul wrote: "O Timothy, keep that which is committed to thy trust, avoiding profane and vain babblings, and oppositions of science falsely so called: Which some professing have erred concerning the faith" (1 Tim. 6:20, 21). "Thou therefore, my son, be strong in the grace that is in Christ Jesus. And the things that thou hast heard of me among many witnesses, the same commit thou to faithful men, who shall be able to teach others also" (2 Tim. 2:1, 2). Our "academic freedom" must always be in bondage to the Bible. I like the New International Version translation of Colossians 2:8: "See to it that no one takes you captive through hollow and deceptive philosophy, which depends on human tradition and the basic principles of this world rather than on Christ." In our Sunday Schools, in our Christian day schools, in our college and seminary classrooms we must always be busily "Casting down imaginations, and every high thing that exalteth itself against the knowledge of God, and bringing into captivity every thought to the obedience of Christ" (2 Cor. 10:5).

Our GARBC will remain strong if we faithfully maintain separatist attitudes, sanctified associations, spiritual ambitions, Scriptural affirmations, strong affections, sacred activities and sound academics. May our God be glorified as we do.

8

New Evangelicalism

SOMEONE HAS astutely observed that a label can often be a libel. Through the centuries Christendom has had plenty of labels and libels. Our own twentieth century has had a proliferation of labels. Modernists and fundamentalists, liberals and conservatives, neoorthodox and evangelicals, new evangelicals and separatists are some of the labels given to various groups in Christendom. The labels, when used accurately, precisely, honestly and definitively, are helpful when identifying a particular person or group. The problems and confusion come when labels are loosely used and inappropriately applied.

In this chapter I would like to deal with new evangelicalism. Too often in recent years we separatists have carelessly labeled anything or anyone with whom we disagree as **new evangelical.** Perhaps Shakespeare would have written: "To label or libel—that is the question!" Seriously, it is vitally important that we carefully and factually apply our labels. To specify critically is one thing; to slander carelessly is quite another. Confusion can only result from imprudent indictments and indiscreet identifications of fellow believers. It is clear from even a cursory review of fundamentalist writings that many men and institutions are being wrongly labeled "new evangelical" when in reality they are not.

Years ago Dr. George Dollar rightly and accurately divided fundamentalists into militants and moderates. He referred to new evangelicals as modified fundamentalists (see *A History of Fundamentalism* by George W. Dollar, published by Bob Jones University Press, Greenville, SC 29614). Such designations distinguish between fundamentalists (militants and moderates) and new evangelicals. There is a great deal of difference between a moderate fundamentalist and a new evangelical, and that difference should not be lightly overlooked. You and I may wish that Moody Bible Institute took the same militant stance as fundamentalist Baptist Bible College of Pennsylvania, but it is not right to classify moderate Moody with new evangelical Fuller Seminary. You and I may wish that John MacArthur were a dyed-in-the-wool Regular Baptist, but it is wrong to label IFCA MacArthur with New Evangelicals like Billy Graham and Leighton Ford. A fundamentalist is not a new evangelical. I surely wish that some fundamentalists were more militant and more aggressively separatist, but I have no right to label or libel a man who holds to the fundamentals of the faith and who is opposed to new evangelicalism's concessions and compromises as a "new evangelical." It does harm to the cause of our militant fundamentalism when we are imprecise in our labels. For that reason we seek herewith to properly describe and define new evangelicalism, which is a real enemy of Biblical fundamentalism.

New Evangelicalism—Compromise with Liberalism

Regular Baptist Press has published a very important book which every reader of these lines ought to purchase and peruse prayerfully: *Neoevangelicalism Today* by Robert P. Lightner. On page 112, Lightner says the following about the new evangelical: "There is a desire to please the liberal, not by denying any of the cardinal doctrines of the fundamentalist but by being less polemic and more positive and loving. The assumption is that the time is ripe for mutual confession of the past and for the sharing of theological viewpoints so that orthodoxy may become less objectionable to those outside its ranks. Worthy as this ambition may be, it is beset with serious difficulties." On pages 132 and 133, Lightner writes: "The usual neoevangelical evaluation of liberalism gives the impression that the battle between truth and error is over. While admitting certain basic fallacies in the new liberal approach, there seems to be an undefined acceptance of the liberal's 'conversion' in other areas. Language which speaks highly of liberalism and neoorthodoxy and decries fundamentalism leaves the layman with a false impression. Neoevangelicals speak frequently of the decay of the Wellhausen hypothesis and the return to Biblical theology. In surveys of the change which world conditions and neoorthodoxy brought upon liberalism, they speak optimistically of many who genuinely returned to a conservative faith. Further adding to the unrealistic optimism is the appearance of articles such as 'Orthodox Agony in the World Council,' 'Evangelical Penetration of the WCC' and 'Evangelical Gains in WCC' in *Christianity Today*. Again, such articles imply to the uninformed layman the 'victories' of evangelicalism. He is led to believe that evangelicalism has finally triumphed and succeeded in converting its opponents, and of course, this is not an accurate picture."

New Evangelicalism—Conformity to Inclusivism

One example of new evangelical inclusivism was the American Festival of Evangelism in Kansas City, July 27-30, 1981. That conclave promoted cooperation among denominational bodies without any concern for what those denominations may or may not teach with reference to the fundamentals of Biblical Christianity. One of the members of the festival's executive committee, Dr. Thomas F. Zimmerman, general superintendent of the Assemblies of God, was interviewed on the occasion of the fortieth anniversary year of the National Association of Evangelicals. Dr. Zimmerman was the tenth president of the NAE (1960-62). He served as chairman of the planning committee of the American Festival of Evangelism. The interview appeared on pages 11 and 12 of the Summer 1981 edition of the NAE magazine, *United Evangelical Action*. Ponder Zimmerman's answers to two questions as evidence of new evangelicalism's conformity to inclusivism. "Question: How do you perceive NAE's role in the future? Answer: I feel that if NAE is to continue to have a breadth of influence and ministry, it must first recognize that there are evangelicals in practically every one of today's organized groups. We need to develop our perspective in such a way that we see the many areas in which we can work with other groups on a given task.

Question: Like? Answer: Like the American Festival of Evangelism. This is the broadest based relationship of churches and church agencies that I suppose has ever worked together on a common effort. And happily, NAE is well represented in the Festival's program leadership." Such unscriptural inclusivism and cooperative compromise is strictly forbidden in 2 Corinthians 6:14-18 and 2 John 7-11.

New Evangelicalism—Criticism of Literalism

Fundamentalists accept Genesis literally. We believe God literally created a literal Adam and a literal Eve. They were real, historical people, not symbols or myths. We believe the Noahic flood was a literal, universal deluge just as the Bible says. New evangelicals are openly critical of such literalism. They are willing to "rethink" Genesis 1-3 in the "light" (how about smog?) of "modern scientific data." *Is the Bible a Human Book?* was published in 1970 by the Broadman Press. The compilers and editors of this volume's essays were Wayne Ward of Southern Baptist Seminary in Louisville and Joseph F. Green. In the chapter entitled "The Bible and Human Science," new evangelical John M. Lewis, pastor of the First Baptist Church of Raleigh, North Carolina, wrote: "Many Bible students realize that there are two accounts of creation in Genesis . . . The older account in Genesis 2 is more primitive and childlike in its concepts and picturizations of God. Here man is created before any other living creatures. This latter story from the Hebrew writer again marks a tremendous advance in the scientific understanding of ancient man. If one tries to take these (creation) accounts as literal scientific truth he does violence to the real intent of the Bible itself. It is a drastic mistake to make the limited science of the Biblical writer part of the revelation of himself which God is giving. If one does this, later scientific discoveries will undermine trust in the Bible as a book of truth. The church assumed, falsely, that Darwin's theory undermined the Biblical story of creation of man. Unfortunately, this still presents a problem for those who cannot distinguish between the process and the purpose of creation" (pp. 96-98). **No fundamentalist, militant or moderate, would ever accept such a betrayal of the book of Genesis.**

In contending for the literalness of Genesis 6—9, Dr. M. R. DeHaan wrote: "Although men have scoffed at the story of the Ark and ridiculed the revelation as utterly absurd, yet if these critics would use their heads before they open their mouths, they would see what fools they were making of themselves. The higher critics call themselves the intelligentsia and look with pity upon us poor, ignorant Bible-believing Christians as being dumb and gullible. But surely the wisdom of man is foolishness with God. Imagine a mere man criticizing the blueprint of Almighty God, the Creator of the universe, and saying that the great God Who designed and planned a universe doesn't know how to build a little boat 450 feet long. Oh, the pathetic, utter stupidity of unbelief! It reminds me of the definiton of a 'higher critic' that I heard the late Dr. A. C. Gabelein give. He said, 'They should be called higher crickets, for they make a lot of noise but are always in the dark.' " (M. R. DeHaan, *The Days of Noah* [Grand Rapids: Zondervan Publishing], p. 164.)

New Evangelicalism—Concession of Inerrancy

Make no mistake about it! The battle in Christendom today is over the inerrancy of the Word of God as originally given. New evangelicalism has lost that battle. Claiming to believe in Biblical infallibility, new evangelicals have conceded Biblical inerrancy. In his book, *The Battle for the Bible,* Dr. Harold Lindsell has documented the sad and sickening willingness of new evangelicals to give up belief in the inerrancy of God's Word. The GARBC stands unashamedly, unabashedly and unwaveringly for the inerrancy of the Word of God. We believe with all fundamentalists that verbal-plenary inspiration demands inerrancy.

The integrity of the Bible calls for its inerrancy. The infallibility of the Bible necessitates its inerrancy. Our GARBC statement of faith declares: "We believe in the authority and sufficiency of the Holy Bible, consisting of the sixty-six books of the Old and New Testaments, as originally written; that it was verbally and plenarily inspired and is the product of Spirit-controlled men, and therefore is infallible and inerrant in all matters of which its speaks."

There is a great need today for a Biblically balanced,

Scripturally sage, spiritual statesmanship in fundamentalist circles. While we stand guard against new evangelicals who would desert and betray the doctrine of Biblical inerrancy, we must also resist new fundamentalists who would seek to create a new test of fellowship among true fundamentalists, a test that neither our fathers nor their fathers were called upon to meet. I speak of those who would insist upon the so-called *Textus Receptus* as the only satisfactory text-type and the King James Version as the only acceptable translation. In this day when we should be wholeheartedly standing for the grand standard of Biblical inerrancy, let us not allow ourselves as fundamentalists to be drawn away to a fuss over translations and/or a debate over Erasmus vs. Westcott and Hort. We would do well to heed the wise words of Dr. Kenneth I. Brown, Dean of the Detroit Baptist Theological Seminary: "The TR defenders hold strongly to the Textus Receptus as the best, in fact the only, text-type. Most of the leading fundamental writers and scholars through the years have not held this to be so. Nearly all of the fundamental men who have written materials dealing with the New Testament prefer the Alexandrian text-type. The reasons for this are sound textually. Those who accept the Alexandrian text-type are not radical, apostate nor heretical. Actually, this position better represents the center of Biblical scholarship and orthodox Christianity. It certainly provides basic answers to some difficult doctrinal matters which otherwise face difficulty in proper exegesis and interpretation. There seems to be no valid reason why the serious student of the New Testament should not use with profit several translations, each with value in its own strength. Defense of the Textus Receptus does not represent the center and heart of Christianity. Such a defense need not be pursued." (Kenneth I. Brown, *A Critical Evaluation of the Text of the King James Bible,* [Detroit Baptist Theological Seminary], pp. 28, 29.) Fundamentalists, therefore, must resist both the new evangelicals and the new fundamentalists if we would clearly, courageously and consistently define and defend the cardinal doctrine of Biblical inerrancy.

New Evangelicalism—Commendation of Charismatics

Perhaps the best known illustration of the commendation

of charismatics by new evangelicals is the willingness of Billy Graham to aid and abet Oral Roberts. The National Association of Evangelicals includes in its membership men and women from seventy denominations. Many of those denominations are charismatic-oriented. "April 3, 1960 is the birthday of the neo-Pentecostal or charismatic movement. On that date Pentecostal teachings began spilling over into non-Pentecostal churches. From that time on Pentecostalism—particularly speaking in tongues—began to be common in all major Protestant denominations. . . . The charismatic movement which claims the revival of the New Testament gifts of tongues and healing is not of God and cannot find Biblical support. It has promoted the liberal ecumenical drive for a one world church since it has swept and continues to sweep both liberal and evangelical churches and organizations" (Robert P. Lightner, *Vital Issues of the Hour in the Light of God's Word*, [Schaumburg: Regular Baptist Press], pp. 40, 48). Instead of denouncing and refuting the unscriptural confusion of the charismatics, new evangelicalism commends it.

New Evangelicalism—Confusion of Church Priorities

What is the work of the Church? Matthew 28:18-20, the Great Commission, makes it clear our responsibility is spiritual, not social. The new evangelicals have increasingly become enamored with the liberal line of "a social conscience." Purely social work is being given an unbiblical prominence in new evangelical circles. Christ called the Church to preach the gospel, disciple converts and plant churches. The Church was never called to make the world a better place in which to live. We do not have a cultural mandate; we do have a Great Commission. Our responsibilities are evangelism and edification, not economics, ecology and environmentalism. The World Evangelical Fellowship and Lausanne Committee for World Evangelization co-sponsored A Consultation on Evangelism and Social Responsibility on June 16-23, 1982, at Reformed Bible College in Grand Rapids, Michigan. Co-chairmen of the meeting were Rev. Gottfried Osei-Mensah of Kenya and Dr. Bong Ro of Taiwan. They are following the leadership of Billy Graham, whose hobnobbing with social-gospel-preachers through the years has helped to add to the confusion. Dr. Ernest Pickering has written: "To find such emphasis upon social action in the teaching of the New Testament would require diligent search and would prove fruitless. Primary place is given to the proclamation of saving grace in Jesus Christ, and the social betterment which surely follows is a by-product but not part of the message. Much of the support for strong social action arises from a misunderstanding and misappropriation of Old Testament passages and excerpts from the Sermon on the Mount" (Ernest Pickering, *Biblical Separation* [Schaumburg: Regular Baptist Press, 1979], p. 134).

New Evangelicalism—Complicity with Romanism

When Billy Graham accepted an honorary degree from a Roman Catholic school, Belmont Abbey College in North Carolina, many evangelicals professed surprise and shock. But Graham was only being consistent with his new evangelical life-style. His romance with Romanism has grown through the years. Moreover, the charismatic movement has furthered relationships between Catholics and new evangelicals. The June 25, 1973, issue of *Newsweek* reported that 22,000 neo-Pentecostals and Catholics gathered at Notre Dame for a charismatic rally. In the September, 1979, *Baptist Bulletin*, in an article entitled "Are Evangelicals Moving Toward Rome?" Dr. Charles U. Wagner said: "Several years ago when I visited the Orient to minister for the Association of Baptists for World Evangelism, I stayed for several nights at a guest house in Japan, something like a motel complex. I discovered that several charismatics were residing there also. The purpose of their being in Tokyo was to hold charismatic meetings in the local Roman Catholic Church. Ironically, while missionaries of ABWE and Baptist Mid-Missions were seeking to liberate people from the awful bondage of Romanism, the charismatics were compromising with the Catholics and holding meetings with them." And so the building of ecumenical bridges between the Vatican and the new evangelicals continues unabated to this hour.

Comments From a Fundamentalist

The label of "new evangelical" should be applied to those

who can be truly identified as new evangelical. We have tried to give seven clear characteristics of such people. The label "new evangelical" should not be applied to just anyone with whom we disagree. The label has to do with far more important issues than just hair lengths, hemlines and harmony lilts. As Dr. Pickering has said, "We must avoid the danger of elevating our own personal tastes or opinions to the level of divine revelation. People with strong convictions (and most separatists are such) have difficulty distinguishing between their opinions and Scriptural principles. In an effort to avoid appearing wishy-washy or uncertain in areas of doctrine, some separatists go to an extreme and take hard, irrevocable stands on every minor issue as though it were a major item of the faith" (Pickering, p. 234). Let us not libel good men with bad labels. Although we may be disappointed at times with the weaknesses of some fundamentalists, let us refrain from labeling them something that does not honestly describe their convictions or positions.

9

The Work of the Pulpit Committee

THERE IS no greater crisis confronting a local Baptist church than that created by a change of pastors. It is imperative that a congregation take every precaution to insure that the right man is called. In the past two years it has been my privilege and responsibility to counsel with many pulpit committees. To my surprise, most men who serve on a pulpit committe have little experience at such work. But such a fact should not be surprising, since pastors do not resign or retire or die that often! I have counseled with men whose pastors have just resigned after more than thirty years in that one pastorate. A number of pulpit committees have talked with me whose pastors have served anywhere from ten to twenty years. And there are many whose pastors have faithfully ministered between five and ten years. So you can see that pulpit committees may not get a whole lot of experience in some churches.

Sometimes bigger churches have less experience at calling a pastor than do smaller ones. Moreover, it has been my observation that too many pulpit committees seem unsure of just how to go about their work. The question has arisen in my mind: Who is responsible for teaching pulpit committees their duties? The answer: the pastor. For that reason, I would like to give you some guidelines for committees who have been charged with the strategic task of searching for a shepherd to lead a local flock. Pulpit committees may be great assets to local churches. They may also be grave liabilities. Since every church will sooner or later need the services of a pulpit committee, every pastor ought to be interested in such committees. If a pastor values his congregation and wants his work to be furthered by his incoming successor, he ought to be vitally and vigorously at work to make sure his future pulpit committee knows what it is doing and how to do it. Competent pulpit committees will ultimately be of great benefit to both churches and pastors. The following ideas are from my heart and head to yours. You may not agree with everything I write on the subject, but I hope and pray you will carefully think through these matters. Perhaps you would like to share this chapter with your board members or at least file it away for future use by your committee when you have resigned, retired or died. (I hope your committee will not be around after the Rapture!)

The Constitution of the Pulpit Committee

Who should serve on a pulpit committee? Before attempting to answer that significant question, let us ponder the words of Edward T. Hiscox: "Great care is needed in the selection of a pastor. Grave interests are committed to his charge, as the religious teacher, leader and example for the flock. Very serious responsibility devolves on the deacons and leading members of the Church especially. An act so vitally connected with the welfare of the cause and the spread of the gospel should be preceded by, and accompanied with, earnest and protracted prayer for divine direction in the choice" (Edward T. Hiscox, *Principles and Practices for Baptist Churches*, Grand Rapids: Kregel Publications, p. 107). The key statement by Hiscox is this: **Very serious responsibility devolves on the deacons and leading members of the Church especially.** Some churches have in recent years felt it necessary to select a pulpit committee comprised of representatives from every phase of church life. They have representatives from the Ladies Missionary Union, the Baptist Youth Group, the Sunday School Board, the Music Committee, the Trustees, the Nursery, etc., etc. While respecting the salutary motivations for such a procedure, I still think it is unwise.

Pulpit committees should be made up of the most spiritual and wise men in the church. I personally believe that the best pulpit committee is the board of deacons, and there are clear Scriptural qualifications for such men (see 1 Timothy 3:8-13). Surely pulpit committee members ought to be "men of honest report, full of the Holy [Spirit] and wisdom . . ." (Acts 6:3). Too often our local church elections are "beauty contests" or "talent contests" when they ought to be sober and prayerful times of choosing men whose lives are clearly Scriptural and consistently spiritual. Men who are to listen discerningly to preachers and whose responsibility is to evaluate pastoral competence should be themselves men of spiritual health and Scriptural holiness.

The pulpit committee should be constituted of men who are vitally aware of what is involved in the pulpit and pastoral ministries of a local church. There should be men on the committee who have *theological discernment*. A Regular Baptist pulpit committee ought to be looking for a Regular Baptist. Churches are surely shortchanged when no one on a pulpit committee knows the difference between a fundamentalist and a new evangelical, or the difference between a pre-trib and a post-trib, or the difference between Baptist immersion and trine immersion. Pulpit committees ought to recognize a Baptist when they talk to one, and they ought to be able to spot an interdenominationalist when they hear him. There should be men on the pulpit committee who have *homiletical discrimination*. Is the man behind the pulpit an expository preacher or an expandatory promoter? Is he throwing light on the Scripture or creating heat? Does he feed or fuss? Will his preaching teach the saints and reach the lost? These questions are crucial and can only be properly answered by people who appreciate good preaching and are able to recognize it when they hear it. There should be men on the pulpit committee who have *evangelistic disposition*. Our churches need pastors who love people and whose hearts are burdened for lost souls. Our churches need men who have such hearts and can detect such soul-winning passion in the person of a prospective candidate. Surely all men who serve on pulpit committees should be characterized by *pastoral devotion*. No man ought to be on a pulpit committee who "has it in" for pastors, who has a carnal hostility to preachers. Pulpit committees ought to be made up of men who respect the God-ordained pastoral office and who also have genuine affection for men of God who teach and preach the Word of God.

The Commitment of the Pulpit Committee

Let's face it! Serving on a pulpit committee is hard work. Those who accept this task must commit themselves to many hours of meetings, prayer, correspondence and travel if the work is to be rightly done. First, there must be **a commitment to travel.** I personally believe it is a mistake for pulpit committees to turn into "tape worms." It is absolutely unfair to the church and to pastors to evaluate and pass judgment on a man on the basis of a tape recording. Cassette tapes don't smile. Or frown! Tapes don't shake hands or look you in the eye. Or evade your eyes. Tapes don't answer questions and reply to problems. Tapes do not introduce their wives and children. Tapes don't smell good. Or have B.O.! Tapes just cannot properly and fairly convey the personality or lack of it, the passion or lack of it, the power or lack of it of the pastor under consideration. Pulpit committees dare not take the easy and unsafe route of depending on tapes. They must travel. If a pulpit committee really wants to see and hear a man as he is, let them travel to where he is currently ministering. There they can observe him as he mingles with the people in the church lobby, as he meets and talks with children and teenagers, as he listens to the elderly, as he makes the announcements from the pulpit, as he prays, as he takes the offering, as he preaches, as he gives the invitation. More can be learned in that two-hour Sunday morning visit than can be gleaned from a half dozen tapes and a twenty-question resume form. Travel! I think it wise for a pulpit committee to spend at least what the pastor's salary would be for travel expenses each week. After all, the church is not expending that amount now for salary; so the committee should put the money to good use and attend the services of men they are seriously considering. If a pulpit committee of six men divided into twos, they could visit three churches in one week.

Second, there must be **a commitment to toleration.** No

man should serve on a pulpit committee if he is unwilling to listen to and respect others. Remember, a pulpit committee is looking for God's man. That man may not meet a particular member's preconceived idea of what the next pastor ought to look like and sound like. The choosing of a pastor is not a simple matter of satisfying one man's desires. Toleration is invaluable to a pulpit committee. First impressions may be lasting; but, then again, they may not be accurate. Some men are naturally attracted to comets, but a steady lamp may be what the church really needs. Some may be impressed by a fireball when what the church may need most is a faithful, warming flame. One member of the committee may want to find a "carbon copy" of the last pastor when what the church needs is a truly "new broom." Saul's armor may need to be traded in for David's slingshot. The evangelist may need to be followed by the expositor or vice versa. If all the members of the committee are tolerant and teachable, there will be ultimate triumph.

Third, there must be **a commitment to trust.** An excellent passage for pulpit committees is James 1:5-8: "If any of you lack wisdom, let him ask of God, that giveth to all men liberally, and upbraideth not; and it shall be given him. But let him ask in faith, nothing wavering. For he that wavereth is like a wave of the sea driven with the wind and tossed. For let not that man think that he shall receive anything of the Lord. A double minded man is unstable in all his ways." Searching for a pastor should be spiritual work, and pulpit committees should be men who have truly prayed for God's direction. They must then genuinely trust Him for that guidance. There will be times of discouragement, times when the congregation will become impatient, and times when your "choice" decides he is to stay where he is. At such times there must be a solid commitment to trust the Lord through it all. Samuel worked his way through all of Jesse's sons, but we are all glad he waited patiently and trustingly for God's man, David. Dr. Paul R. Jackson has wisely written: "The committee must be very careful to avoid even the appearance of trying to railroad some man into the church. It must also refuse to yield to personal desires, personal friends or pressure groups that may appear. This work must be a sincere, prayerful effort to find a real man of God who can effectively minister the Word of God and pastor the flock of God" (Paul R. Jackson, *The Doctrine and Administration of the Church* [Schaumburg: Regular Baptist Press, 1968], p. 56).

The Consultations of the Pulpit Committee

Years ago Dr. Robert T. Ketcham wrote a little paper entitled *Your Next Pastor*. He asked: "Whom could the pulpit committee consult?" His answer was fivefold: (1) the National Representative; (2) the chairman or members of the state council in your area; (3) the state missionary or representative; (4) pastors in other GARBC churches; (5) one or more of our approved schools or missions. Certainly Proverbs 11:14 is applicable here: "Where no counsel is, the people fall: but in the multitude of counsellors there is safety." Recognizing this, my predecessors in the office of National Representative established the practice of writing a letter to churches when they became pastorless. Originally composed by Dr. Ketcham and used also by Dr. Jackson and Dr. Stowell and now by me, the letter says in part: "According to our records here in the home office your church is either pastorless or about to become so. Your staff here in the office wishes to offer itself to you and your church for any service we may render in helping you to find God's man for your next pastor. Please understand that you are perfectly free to pursue your task without our help. Yours is a sovereign, local Baptist church in fellowship with the General Association of Regular Baptist Churches. You are the ones to judge and decide whether or not you desire our help. All we can do is offer it. . . . We have sat here in the office and watched churches call men whom we knew had a record of church wrecking, careless personal living and unbiblical and unbaptistic views. In every case we have had to sit silently by and helplessly watch this situation develop. We believe here that a Baptist church is sovereign and no outsider has any right to intrude into its affairs. If such a church would write or contact this office, then we would be perfectly free to advise them. But until and unless it does contact us, we are helpless to do anything about it."

Pulpit committees who isolate themselves from the advice and counsel of others are not wise. Dr. Paul R. Jackson candidly wrote: "Many men who seek pastorates are unqualified or unworthy for such ministry, and no one should be called who has not been thoroughly investigated. . . . His past record should be checked and detailed questions asked. No man worthy of such a position would object to a thorough investigation" (Jackson, pp. 53, 54). Hiscox, in his aforementioned book, concurs when he says: "In calling a man to the pastorate, the Church should take deliberate care to know his *record;* what he has done elsewhere, and how he is esteemed and valued where he has previously lived and labored. It is a piece of reckless folly, of which churches are often guilty—and for which they justly suffer—that on the credit of a few flashy or fascinating sermons, wholly ignorant of his private character and of his ministerial history, they call and settle a pastor. . . . If the churches wish to avoid men unsuited to them, and especially if they wish to escape the plague of unworthy men in their pulpits, they must use more caution in the calling and settlement of pastors" (Hiscox pp. 108, 109). In other words, **if you want the right result, consult!**

The Candidates and the Pulpit Committee

Once the pulpit committee has become serious enough about a prospective pastor to talk with him, what should be on the agenda to discuss? Two primary topics are **the candidate** and **the church.** The committee should ask questions of the candidate, but committee members must also be prepared to answer honestly and forthrightly questions the candidate will ask about the church.

With reference to **the candidate,** let me suggest eight areas for productive probing: (1) Doctrine. Be as detailed as possible. The candidate should have been given a copy of the articles of faith well in advance of the meeting. Ask the candidate if he has any disagreements whatsoever with that doctrinal statement. (2) Education. What schools did he attend? Is he now a student? Has he a good and growing library? Does he study and read? (3) Position. Is he a Baptist by conviction? Ask him to name the Baptist distinctives. If he has pastored other than Baptist churches, ask why he did. (4) Separation. Ask him to define his convictions on ecclesiastical and personal separation. Probe his viewpoints on the charismatic movement, ecumenical evangelism and new evangelicalism. (5) Associations. Is he in full agreement with the position of the GARBC? Will he work enthusiastically with the state association of Regular Baptist churches? Does he actively encourage area Regular Baptist pastors with his presence and fellowship at their meetings? (6) Spirituality. Ask about his private prayer and devotional life. Is he burdened for souls? Is he head of his home? Is his wife happy? Are his children obedient? (7) Conditions. Discuss openly and thoroughly his salary and housing needs, vacation time, annual GARBC and state conference arrangements, moving mode and expense allowance, possible time of arrival on the field and fringe benefits such as hospitalization and retirement program. Be prepared to negotiate if his needs are greater than you anticipated. (8) Goals. Ask the prospective pastor what his goals would be for himself and the church were he called. Preaching goals. Sunday School attendance goals. Church attendance goals. Missionary budget goals. Building and equipment goals. Financial goals. Organizational goals. Overall spiritual goals. Find out if the man has vision and ambition and plans.

With reference to **the church,** the pulpit committee must be prepared to inform the candidate on some strategic matters about the local church. (1) Opportunity. Is the community stagnant, dying or growing? What is the building situation? Is the present facility landlocked? Is there any room for expansion? Would relocation be an acceptable option? (2) Deacons. How do they see themselves with reference to the pastor? Are they pastor-boosters? What is their devotional life? Do they call? Are they burdened for souls? Are their wives and children in proper subjection? Do they attend prayer meeting regularly? Are all of them tithers? (3) Sunday School. Is it growing? Is there a teacher-training program? Are there standards for all teachers and superintendents? What type of records are kept? Are Regular Baptist Press materials and take-home papers used in all departments? (4) Budget. How much for general expenses? How much for missions? What indebtedness does the church have? Answer all these questions honestly. If your church has problems, say so! The "problem solver" may be that very candidate before you.

When you invite the candidate to preach, have him come for at least a Sunday through a Wednesday so your people can really get to know him and his wife. Finally, heed the wise words of R. T. Ketcham in "Your Next Pastor": "Do not vote on more than one candidate at a time. Worthy pastors do not like to be participants in a 'ministerial beauty contest.' Very good men may not permit themselves to be considered if they are to be placed in competition with fellow pastors."

10

The Place of the Sunday School

RECENTLY I read the biography of one of the great Baptist leaders of the nineteenth century, Benjamin Griffith. His mother died when he was only three weeks old. At the age of eleven he was left an orphan by the death of his father in March of 1833. The turning point of his life came when he was invited to the Sunday School of the First Baptist Church in Baltimore, Maryland. At the age of eighteen he accepted Christ as his personal Savior and a few months later began to prepare for the pastoral ministry at Madison (now Colgate) University. After fruitful ministries in churches in Cumberland, Maryland, and Philadelphia, Pennsylvania, Griffith in 1857 became the Executive Editor of the then thirteen-year-old American Baptist Publication Society. For the next thirty-six years until his death in October of 1893, Benjamin Griffith was one of the mightiest men of God in America in the work of Baptist Sunday Schools. His biographer tells us Griffith "sought to have Sunday Schools so planted that they might naturally grow into churches." And it was a great joy to him that the Society's agents, during the period of his official management, organized nearly ten thousand Sunday Schools, out of which grew more than a thousand churches! "He believed in the Sunday School. He sought to promote it, not because he was officially required to do so, but because he believed in it, and personally loved it." So wrote Griffith's biographer in 1894.

What Benjamin Griffith loved and promoted one hundred years ago must be loved and promoted by Regular Baptists now. Declining attendance has characterized American Sunday Schools of all denominations and associations for the past five years. We must reverse that trend in the General Association of Regular Baptist Churches. Sanctified adaptability, innovation and planned hard work can once again get our Sunday Schools moving ahead to grow and glow for God.

The Sunday School's Significance

What Robert Raikes began in 1780 had grown to worldwide proportion by the time of his death in 1811. He had worked tirelessly to prove the validity and value of the Sunday School. He was still actively involved in the work when, at the age of seventy-five, he went home to be with the Lord. Two hundred years after the birth of the Sunday School as we know it, we must ask the question: Is the Sunday School still significant? I believe it is! Dr. Charles U. Wagner has written: "Pastors and Christian workers will agree that a well-administered Sunday School can be one of the greatest boons to the church. . . . Because most of our missionaries and pastors (85% of them!) come up through the Sunday School, it is important that the pastor stress at the outset his concern for the Sunday School and its rightful place in the church" (Charles U. Wagner, *The Pastor: His Life and Works* [Schaumburg: Regular Baptist Press, 1976], pp. 216, 217). The significance of the Sunday School is further highlighted by Dr. Ruth C. Haycock: "The Sunday School, in addition to having the longest history of any church educational agency, is also the most comprehensive. In Bible-believing churches, it has the largest attendance, covers the widest span of years, has available the richest curriculum resources, is graded most carefully, and has the most influence on the church's decisions about facilities. . . . Though there have been critics of the Sunday School, God has honored and used it to the salvation and spiritual growth of multitudes" (Robert E. Clark and Roy B. Zuck, eds., *Childhood Education in the Church* [Chicago: Moody Press], pp. 316, 317).

The Sunday School's Shepherd

Churches with growing Sunday Schools have pastors who are vitally involved in the promotion, planning and perspiration of the Sunday School. In his aforementioned book, Dr. Wagner declares: "Benson points out that it is significant that the French Commission considered the Sunday School 'an absolute necessity for the complete instruction of the child.' Because we believe this is true, it is vitally important that the pastor take the leadership in the Sunday School administration. He should see that adults and children get the maximum benefit from the Sunday School. . . . One of the major goals emphasized from the platform should be the growth and progress of the Sunday School. . . . The pastor should keep the work and the goals of the Sunday School before the people constantly and show, both in his message and practice, his interest in it" (Wagner, pp. 216-220). Sunday School must be exciting to the pastor if it is to be exciting to the congregation.

Churches with growing Sunday Schools have pastors who give top priority to the work of the Sunday School. There is a limit to time and personnel in every church. Growing churches and Sunday Schools are those that give top priority to the Sunday services of the church. Sunday School, Morning Worship, Evening Worship and Midweek Prayer Meeting occupy the greatest amount of the time and personnel of strong churches and pastors. If you are going to build a strong local church and Sunday School, you must not allow your people's energies to be dissipated by all kinds of extra-church and para-church programs and activities. Priorities must be set. Personnel must be mobilized.

The Sunday School's Superintendency

No man in the congregation is as valuable to the pastor as is the Sunday School superintendent. In too many churches that strategic office is filled by an election between two men who are secretly praying that the other one gets elected (smile!). Seriously, all too often the critical leadership position of Sunday School superintendent is no more than a "beauty contest" between two men who have no yen for the work at all. Surely it is to the advantage of the church when the pastor is free to choose his own Sunday School superintendent, a man with whom he will work closely, compatibly and constructively.

In the introduction to his excellent book, *Superintend with Success,* Dr. Guy P. Leavitt has written: "Business has what it calls the four 'izes' of good management: Visualize, Organize, Deputize and Supervise. To these I have added a fifth: Analyze. The Sunday School is the biggest business on earth and produces the world's finest product—a Christian. The superintendent is called upon to employ these 'izes.' " (Guy P. Leavitt, *Superintend with Success* [Cincinnati: Standard Publishing Co.], p. 5). Dr. Leavitt recommends one-year terms: "Since there is much to learn in order to be a successful superintendent, and since experience is the best training, the superintendent is returned to office year after year. . . . When the school ceases to thrive under the leadership, the annual choice offers a convenient opportunity for the change" (Leavitt, p. 28). How we need to pray for a mighty army of consecrated Sunday School superintendents with the same burden that drove businessman Robert Raikes!

The Sunday School's Staff and Standards

According to Dr. Earle G. Griffith, "Not a few Sunday Schools are either counterfeit or competitive churches in disguise. It would be better to have no Sunday School than to have one that turns attention from the church and devitalizes it. A good practice in a well-organized Sunday School is to insist that leaders, teachers and secretaries be members of the local church. It ought to be obvious that all should be forthright Christians in their convictions, character and conduct . . . the entire staff of workers should accept unconditionally the doctrines and practices of the church. The teachers and officers of their own accord should set up and gladly maintain Bible standards of life and ministry" (Earle G. Griffith, *The Pastor As God's Minister* [Schaumburg: Regular Baptist Press, 1977]. pp. 193, 194).

The great challenge which faces the teacher is expressed by Guy P. Leavitt: "You as a teacher must be intellectually alert because you have such a short time in which to teach. In one year your pupils spend less time in Bible study class than the equivalent of two weeks in public school. If a public school teacher were asked to do a year's work of English literature, or social studies, or math in two weeks, he would declare it to be impossible. Yet you, as a Sunday School teacher, are asked to teach the Bible, Christian history, Christian doctrine, and an understanding of the relation of the Christian faith to all things in life, and do it in those few, brief hours" (Guy P. Leavitt, *Teach with Success* [Cincinnati: Standard Publishing Co.], p. 21).

In order to keep teachers well-prepared and well-motivated, it is necessary to have a carefully planned teacher training program. The general superintendent and department superintendents must make teacher recruitment and teacher training high priorities in their work. Ponder Dr. Leavitt's words: "The most important qualification of a teacher (or any Sunday School worker) is the desire to improve. Possibly the worst affliction of the Sunday School and the entire church is pious self-satisfaction that stagnates the soul. If a church worker, or any Christian, is willing to study and strive for improvement, trusting the Lord for guidance, he or she can succeed. Before a person should be considered as a possible teacher in Sunday School, even though this person has been teaching for years, the willingness and desire to improve should be assured. What we are is God's gift to us. What we become is our gift to Him" (Leavitt, *Superintend with Success*, p. 73).

The Sunday School's Studies

In his above-mentioned book. Dr. Earle G. Griffith has declared: "It is unreasonable, inconsistent and ungenerous for any preacher to argue that neither teacher nor pupil in the Sunday School should be supplied with any printed material other than the Bible. As certainly as expositiory and research books are of value to a minister of the gospel, they are beneficial to teachers and pupils. It is their proper right to have such; but when we assemble in our schools on the Lord's Day, it should be to study the Bible" (Griffith, p. 192). Dr. Ruth C. Haycock concurs: "The choice of a Sunday School curriculum is of utmost concern. Both teachers and pupils learn Bible content and doctrine largely through this curriculum. A good curriculum should, therefore, be thoroughly Biblical, agree with the church's doctrine, be carefully graded, and furnish the teacher with helps adequate for a well-conducted class. The major purpose of the Sunday School is to teach the Word of God in order that lives may be changed. Thorough Bible instruction will result in worship, expression and service. If instruction does not lead to such response, it is incomplete" (Clark and Zuck, *Childhood Education in the Church*, p. 316).

The Sunday School's Situation

By "situation" I mean building facilities. One Christian educator has rightly said Sunday School facilities should be concerned with **ventilation, illumination and communication.** We need to breathe well, see well and hear well when in Sunday School. A Sunday School room should not have a great deal in common with a locker room! Dr. Leavitt writes: "If your church does not have a Sunday School building, or wing, usually called the educational plant, you probably are planning one. So important does the church consider its school that such an educational plant is often erected before there is an auditorium for the worshipers. This has become perhaps the most significant change in church building in the present century. For such buildings careful planning is necessary. Usually there is a 'Master Plan' for the church property as a whole. The Sunday School building is part of that plan. If may be a separate structure or it may be part of the one main church building. It may even be several buildings. . . . When the school is departmentalized, the building should be constructed with departments rather than for single, separate classes. The reasons for this are obvious" (Leavitt, *Superintend with Success*, p. 125).

The Sunday School's Students

Sunday School is for everybody! We never outgrow our need for Bible study. A strong Sunday School will have a strong adult department. Dr. Wagner has written: ". . . balance is important. It is regrettable that many churches have been given a 'black eye' because of the tremendous growth of the Sunday School with an imbalanced proportion of boys and girls. I am not suggesting by this that the Sunday School should not reach as many boys and girls as possible; but when a church has as many as twelve or thirteen hundred in Sunday School, with only five percent of that number being adults, it is out of balance. This calls for an examination of goals and direction of effort. While growth is important, care must be taken not to place more emphasis on making records than on reaching the people in the community.

It is imperative that both adults and children be sought and brought into the Sunday School. All efforts should be given to attaining a healthy balance in this respect. A Sunday School which grows steadily and maintains its growth through vigorous visitation and compassionate concern will be more stable than one which relies on 'Madison Avenue' gimmicks" (Wagner, p. 220). The pastor must constantly and ceaselessly encourage the adults to be regular in Sunday School attendance. To help you to do this, the late Dr. Fred M. Barlow, Sunday School Consultant for RBP, authored an excellent book which may be ordered from Regular Baptist Press. It is *Vitalizing Your Sunday School Visitation*. This book is full of practical helps.

Another area for outreach has to do with special people like the retarded and deaf. Many of our churches have a Sunday School class for retarded people called "The Shepherd's Class," named after our home for the mentally retarded in Union Grove, Wisconsin. Roberta L. Graff has written: "Every year approximately 130,000 babies are born in the United States with some degree of mental retardation. In Canada, approximately 17,000 babies each year are born retarded. In both countries, 3 percent of the population are retarded. In the U.S., this is 6½ million people—twice as many as those who are affected by blindness, polio, cerebral palsy and heart disease combined. . . . The church can help meet the spiritual needs of retarded children in a way that no community program can possibly do. A concerned parent has suggested two specific ways in which local churches can minister to retardates. First, churches realizing that the retarded are individuals for whom Christ died can provide classes in Sunday School and Vacation Bible School. . . . Second, churches can show concern for each retardate's family members" (Clark and Zuck, pp. 426, 427).

Still another mission field is the deaf population. Dr. Cathy Rice, widow of the founder of the Bill Rice Ranch in Murfreesboro, Tennessee, the world's largest missionary work to the deaf, has written a tremendously useful book entitled *Sign Language for Everyone: A Basic Course in Communication with the Deaf.* In the foreword of this 172-page book, Don Cabbage says; "The deaf population in the United States today nearly equals the population of Canada, numbers more than all the inhabitants of the Caribbean Islands, and has been growing at an ever-increasing rate for several years. For the Christian, these facts should strike a responsive chord. 'How shall they believe in him of whom they have not heard?' " (Rom. 10:14).

Sunday Schools of the GARBC, arise! Let's make the words "Bring Them In" more than musical lyrics. Let's reach and teach as never before for the eternal glory of our great God and Savior, Jesus Christ.

11

Evangelistic Outreach, Not Politics

ON PAGE 69 of the March 22, 1982, issue of *Newsweek*, Kenneth L. Woodward wrote: "For 40 years, evangelist Billy Graham has doggedly pursued the Apostles' 'great commission' to carry the Gospel to the ends of the earth. But there is one country where Graham has never been allowed to preach: the Soviet Union. Now Billy has that chance. *Newsweek* has learned that several weeks ago Graham received an unprecedented invitation from Patriarch Pimen, the head of the Russian Orthodox Church, to preach in Moscow's Patriarchal Cathedral on May 9. The church service will open a Soviet-sponsored conference on 'the preservation of life from nuclear destruction,' which Graham has also been invited to attend as an American observer. Since such conferences are always tightly controlled by the Kremlin, Reagan Administration officials believe the Soviets are trying to manipulate the evangelist for propaganda purposes. At the behest of White House national-security adviser William Clark, Vice-President George Bush personally telephoned Graham while he was in London recently to urge him not to go. At the same time, a number of influential evangelicals in Congress, including senators Mark Hatfield of Oregon and Jesse Helms of North Carolina, have been encouraging him to make the trip—and Graham intimates predict that he will go. . . . Since Graham's 1977 evangelical crusade in Hungary, he has increasingly identified himself with Christians and Jews in Eastern Europe—and he has been quietly pressing for an invitation from Moscow. At the same time, Graham has broken with his more conservative evangelical brethren by outspokenly condemning the nuclear-arms race. His private visit with Pope John Paul II last year was devoted almost exclusively to one theme: world peace and the prevention of a nuclear Armageddon. 'If I go to Moscow, I will preach only the Gospel,' Graham insisted to *Newsweek* last week. But that is not what worries U.S. Government officials. They point out that if he accepts the Soviet invitation, he will be preaching on a national holiday that commemorates Russian military victories in World War II. What's more, State Department officials claim that the peace conference Graham would attend has, as always, been rigged. A final resolution praising Soviet peace efforts has already been drafted, and conference rules will prevent delegates from making significant alteration in the text once the meeting is under way."

The *Newsweek* article is further evidence of Billy Graham's sad lack of discernment. Graham did go to Moscow, and his compromise was evident and a great disappointment to Bible-believers who practice Biblical separation. Note that the church service to which Graham was invited to speak was to open a Soviet-sponsored conference. Also note such conferences are always tightly controlled by the Kremlin. And Reagan Administration officials believed the Soviets were trying to manipulate the evangelist for propaganda purposes. So what else is new? For thirty years Graham has been manipulated. The religious liberals have manipulated him and used his so-called crusades to further denominational infidelity and the ecumenical movement. The Roman Catholics have manipulated him to further the cause of Pope John Paul's false teaching. If then Vice-President Bush had succeeded in convincing Graham "the end does not justify the means" when those "means" are unwise and unscriptural, Bush would have been more persuasive and successful than have been Bob Jones, Sr., and Dr. Robert T. Ketcham in past years and a host of present fundamental leaders. True-to-the-Bible fundamentalists have begged Graham for three decades to cease and desist in his ecumenical evangelism, to no avail. He has worked with liberals, with Catholics and now with Communists. "Billy Graham has been destroying the wall of separation that should have existed between light and darkness. The result—a blending of God's people with the unregenerate and that in willful ignorance and open denial of the warnings from both modern and medieval history. Evangelical-Romanist evangelism pictures as liars those scholars who have described the doctrines and history of Rome; its cooperation with Romanism mocks the choice of millions who refused to cooperate and chose rather to suffer martyrdom at the hand of that same organization. It betrays the modern work of those in many lands who seek to lead Roman Catholics to light and truth. Its affiliation with Romanism ridicules the warnings of a holy God when He spoke of that same religious-political system in these words, 'Come out of her, my people, that ye be not partakers of her sins, and that ye receive not of her plagues' (Rev. 18:4)." (Rev. Wilson Ewin, *Evangelism, Our Birthright and Its Betrayal*, p. 13; available from the Canadian Council of Evangelical Protestant Churches, 90 Melford Drive, Unit #8, Scarborough, Ontario, Canada M1B 2A1.)

This unusually long introduction is important background for what I want to herein emphasize. More than ever, the General Association of Regular Baptist Churches must major on missions. But first we must understand what we mean by missions! Billy Graham has confused gospel preaching with "world peace and the prevention of a nuclear Armageddon." But our responsibility is not to espouse a social gospel or to promote a political panacea. Biblical missionary activity has to do with preaching the gospel of Christ, discipling the converts and establishing New Testament local churches. Our job is not to hold "crusades" with infidels, Catholics and Communists as our sponsors; our task is to work with God's people to win the lost and organize them Scripturally into sound churches that will continue to teach the doctrines of the Word of God faithfully. The remainder of this chapter will be concerned with "A Look at the World," "A Look at the Word" and "A Look at the Work." Most of our space will be devoted to "A Look at the World."

A Look at the World

Our Lord commanded: ". . . Lift up your eyes, and look

on the fields; for they are white already to harvest" (John 4:35). A world of almost five billion people must be seen! We preachers must see it. We must show it to our people. We must prayerfully urge our young people to look on the fields. That is why I want to give you some helpful information. Let's look at our world! Let's look at some of the strategic countries which may hold the key to the evangelizing of the rest of our world.

Argentina. This nation of more than 32 million people is surely one of the great mission fields of South America. The great metropolis of Buenos Aires should challenge the hearts of many young men in our churches, colleges and seminaries. What a fertile field for the planting of New Testament churches!

Australia. Teeming cities like Melbourne, Sidney, Perth and the capital, Canberra, have hardly been touched for our fundamental Baptist movement. The fifteen million people "down under" speak their own unique version of English, but language is really no barrier. What a frontier for church-planting young men with a vision of the future for this resourceful nation.

Austria. Vienna speaks of culture. Innsbruck reminds us of winter sports. But Austria is a nation of 8 million souls and, I believe, a key to the evangelization of Europe. Who will go from our churches to persevere and endure and struggle to overcome the intellectual, materialistic and religious obstacles Satan has erected in that country? Religion is not synonymous with Bible Christianity, and Austria is an example of the disparity.

Belgium. Ten million people live here. The great capital of Brussels is one of the strategic cities of the world. What influence for God a Regular Baptist preacher could have from the pulpit of a strong church in this city! We preachers need to challenge our young men to meet the needs of such areas with the message of the Word of God.

Brazil. Both Baptist Mid-Missions and the Association of Baptists for World Evangelism have labored with stalwart faithfulness in this great South American nation of more than 153 million people. Great, sprawling cities like Rio de Janeiro, Sao Paulo, Recife and the capital, Brasilia, are bursting with business, religion, education and politics. Bible-believing churches are sorely needed. The Mormons have recently applied for 5,000 visas because they realize how crucial Brazil is to all of South America. Oh, that our young men would hear the Macedonian-like call of Brazil—"Come over and help us!"

Chile. In recent years this nation has narrowly escaped the clutches of international communism and anarchy. Almost 13 million people live in Chile, and its capital city of Santiago is surely one of the needy cities of the world. The hold of Roman Catholicism on this country is evidenced by the celebration of two public holidays, August 15 in honor of the bodily assumption of Mary into Heaven, and December 8 in honor of the immaculate conception. How we need to challenge this Romanist bastion with the gospel of grace!

Denmark, Norway, Sweden. Surely the doctrine of permissiveness has had its day in Copenhagen, Denmark and Stockholm, Sweden. Oslo, Norway, a stronghold of Scandinavian religious pride, has relatively few fundamental Baptist works. Nine million Swedes, 4 million Norwegians and 6 million Danes need the gospel. Who will go to them? Perhaps a Johnson or Swanson or Pearson or Nelson or Dahlberg in your church could be challenged to take the Word to his homeland.

Egypt. Sadat is dead! The news sent shock waves around the globe. Politicians trembled. Educators speculated. The free world looked with anxiety while the communist world hoped for some advantage as the new leader of Egypt emerged from the tragedy of the controversial Sadat's death. How should we as Bible-believing Christians see Egypt? The Pharaohs are gone. The Coptic church is bereft of power. Cairo is a stronghold of Islam. And 54 million Egyptians hold the key to the Middle East peace along with Israel. Are we witnessing to Egyptian exchange students while they are in our country? Are we seeking to prepare missionaries to take the gospel to this volatile, difficult land? Is there a modern-day Joseph who will witness of the true God to Egypt's modern-day Pharaoh?

Finland. My good friends, Tom and Linda Ruhkala, are pioneer missionaries to this brave people who have stood up to the Russians more than once. Tom's letters tell of the tremendous difficulties involved in learning the Finnish language. This nation of 5 million people is known primarily by its great capital city of Helsinki. It is a nation with proud traditions and stubborn independency of personality. How the Finns need our Savior!

France. Paris! Romance! Excitement! History! But not many New Testament churches! France, a land of 55 million souls. Cities like Lyons, Marseilles and Nice with little gospel witness and much dead religion. Voltaire once ridiculed Christianity, and his cynical satire is shared by millions of Frenchmen today. The land of the conquering Napoleon needs to be conquered by ambassadors for Christ.

Germany. More than 80 million people live in affluent, reunified Germany. Our Lord said life consisteth not in the abundance of things a man possesses (Luke 12:15), but you will not find many Germans who really believe Him. Our missionaries have found this nation a difficult field in which to serve. The need, however, is not for retreat but for more consecrated laborers.

Ghana. Many are the emerging nations of that great continent, Africa, but none are any more crucial to Africa's well-being than Ghana, a nation of 15 million people. Accra, the capital city, is progressive, influential and open to the gospel. I had great fellowship at Campus Baptist Church with several exchange students at Iowa State University from Ghana. A well-churched Ghana could send many missionaries all over Africa!

India. How can we possibly convey the needs of spiritually impoverished India in a few sentences? Or its importance to Bangladesh and Pakistan? Or its relationship to the Soviet Union and the United States? More than 850 million people, almost three times the population of the U.S.A.! The great population centers of Delhi, Calcutta, Bombay and Madras are teeming with humanity who celebrate Mahatma Gandhi's birthday every October 2. Gandhi was the Indian leader who reportedly said he would have become a Christian had it not been for the Christians he knew. India is still one of the great mission fields of the world.

Indonesia. A nation of 200 million souls. The huge city of Jakarta stands as a challenge to Christianity's dedication to the Great Commission. We must not ignore Indonesia if we are to evangelize that part of the world.

Japan. Toyota! Datsun! Radios! Calculators! Computers! Japan! How those Japanese have challenged us technologically and economically! A nation of more than 120 million people and still open to the work of missionaries. Tokyo, one of the great cities of the world, with very little fundamental Baptist testimony. Who will go? Who will take the challenge of the language? Who will give their lives to win Japanese to Christ? Our bombs destroyed Hiroshima and Nagasaki. Who will take our Bible to bless them?

Mexico. Our neighbor nation of 90 million people is awakening. Mexico City is one of the largest, fastest-growing cities in the world. Our citizens go to Acapulco, Guadalajara, Tijuana and Veracruz to play; maybe we'd better go to pray and preach. Surely we need to plant Baptist churches in this beautiful country just south of the border!

Nigeria. Along with Ghana, Nigeria is one of the key countries of Africa. Almost 120 million people live in this great nation. Lagos is the beautiful captial city. While in Ames, Iowa, I baptized some Nigerian converts into the membership of the Campus Baptist Church. They have since returned to their homeland to help in the establishment of a strong, New Testament church. This country is crucial in the evangelizing of many other African nations. Lagos alone is a staggering challenge.

Philippines. Almost 70 million people are to be found in the Philippines. The Association of Baptists for World Evangelism has seen God work mightily there for some five decades. Some Filipino pastors attended our annual conference in Denver. My daughter, Jill, spent eight weeks in the summer of 1982 in a MAP mission to the Philippines. Manila is the great capital of this brave nation. We need to pray much for the hundreds of Regular Baptist churches there.

Spain. The Spanish Inquisition! Franco! But now the almost 40 million people of Spain have an opportunity to hear the gospel. The capital city of Madrid and other population centers like Barcelona are bombarded with the gospel by Transworld Radio, but now is the time for missionaries to move into this needy nation with literature, love and consecrated lives.

South Africa. This nation of almost 40 million people is experiencing a great deal of unrest. Pretoria, a great capital city, is the object of much political criticism from the black peoples of the earth. Surely this nation needs the gospel now as never before.

United Kingdom. The land of Charles Spurgeon, a mission field? Yes. Sadly, the 60 million people of Queen Elizabeth's United Kingdom are far from the faith of their fathers. London has very few fundamental Baptist churches. England has gone from Bibles to Beatles, and the trip has been tragic. The need for missionaries is acute, and language need not be a barrier.

We have only scratched the surface. Red China with 1 billion souls. Russia with 262 million souls. Yugoslavia, surely a key to Eastern Europe, Tito's domain for so long, with 23 million souls. Tito is gone, but the need is still there. Look on the fields: 4 billion, 400 million souls. By the year 2,000 that population will number 6 billion, 500 million.

A Look at the Word

"But when he saw the multitudes, he was moved with compassion on them, because they fainted, and were scattered abroad, as sheep having no shepherd. Then saith he unto his disciples, The harvest truly is plenteous, but the labourers are few; Pray ye therefore the Lord of the harvest, that he will send forth labourers into his harvest" (Matt. 9:36–38). It is clear the key to worldwide evangelization is **prayer.** That is so because prayer produces **personal revival, personnel recruitment** and **proper results.** We must get our people into serious, sustained, Scriptural intercession for missions. I am particularly exercised that we pray for the primary request: "that he will send forth labourers into his harvest." Are we really praying for our young people by name? Are we asking God to make our teenagers into pastors and missionaries? I know God does not call every Christian young person into the pastorate or onto the mission field, but I am convinced God is calling far more young people into missions than are responding positively to that call! Sure, we need Christian businessmen, computer operators, scientists and lawyers. But I am convinced we need far more missionaries than we are now getting. Our lack of prayer may well be the real reason for our lack of personnel.

A Look at the Work

How many pastors promote missions? Let me suggest you have a "city of the month" or a "country of the month" featured every month in your church bulletin, on your church bulletin board and from the pulpit. I have just listed 23 countries and more than 30 great cities, enough to carry you through two years. Get information and pictures and even slides on each country and burden your young people about the needs there. **Make them aware of a lost world.** Second, pray seriously about starting a branch church. The more churches on the home front, the more support for worldwide missions and the more potential for missionary personnel. Third, send your young people to camp. Through the years the Spirit of God has been pleased to challenge hundreds of young people to service for Christ through the concentrated ministries of our camps.

12

A Look at Mariolatry

IN ALL of my preaching conferences I have said that the four most serious challenges to Bible Christianity are the Mormons, the Moslems, the Mariolaters and the Modernists. It is my firm conviction that Regular Baptists had better focus their spiritual weapons of warfare to the counteracting of those challenges. Religion is rampant around the world. The resurgence of oriental religions is nothing less than astounding. Millions are in the sway of a cultic mentality that is foreign to Bible Christianity. But no challenge to the true faith of the Bible is more subtle and insidious than that of Mariolatry. Make no mistake about it, the Roman Catholic Church is experiencing a renewal around the world. It is being led by one of the most personable, winsome, charisma-coated men of this twentieth century, Pope John Paul II. Everywhere he goes, millions gather to hear him, see him, fawn on him. He has dared to come to the United States; he has made bold to go to England; he has stepped on the soil of nations hitherto hostile to Romanism; and in every instance he has won people to himself and his church. He is the world's best salesman of Mariolatry.

A Papal Ascendancy of Mary

On the front page of the May 14, 1982, edition of *The Scranton Times,* appeared the following headline: "Campaign Making Marian Cult A Cornerstone of Papacy." Under an Associated Press dateline of Fatima, Portugal, the amazing article read as follows: "Pope John Paul II has embarked on a campaign to make the cult of the Virgin Mary a cornerstone of his papacy, rejecting criticism that it delays Christian unity and is a throwback to the Middle Ages. Halfway though his four-day visit to Portugal, the pope has spent almost more time speaking about the mother of Christ than about Christ, Himself. He has credited the 'Queen of Peace' with saving his life from an assassination attempt in St. Peter's Square last year and is visiting three Portuguese shrines dedicated to the Madonna. He prayed silently before her image for half an hour Thursday, kissed her robes and invoked her to convert the Soviets to Christianity, as the three shepherds of Fatima urged after they had visions of the Virgin in 1917. He has even pleaded with the Virgin to save his visit to Britain, May 28, from cancellation by stopping the fighting between Britain and Argentina in the South Atlantic. Christ's mother is revered throughout the Catholic world as a sinless virgin and has inspired hundreds of painters and sculptors through the centuries. But during the 1962-65 Second Vatican Council, liberals tried to block conservative moves to give Mary, who acquired scores of illustrious titles through the ages, an even greater status. The council, reflecting a belief that Marianism can detract from the importance of Christ, decided the church doctrines on Mary ranked lower in the 'hierarchy of truths.' Another brake to veneration of Mary has been Protestant accusations that Rome attaches too much importance to her. A joint Catholic-Anglican commission earlier this year conceded some obstacles to unity still remained in the field of Marian devotion."

How does Pope John Paul II respond to those who would water down Marianism? "The objections do not seem to bother the former Karol Wojtyla, who grew up in Poland without a mother. Since he became bishop of Krakow, his robes have been embroidered with the letter 'M' for Maria. After he became pope, he adopted a blue and white papal shield bearing the letter 'M' in the lower corner. His own motto reproduced in banners greeting him is 'Totus tuus sum Maria'—'Mary, I am all yours.' And he has visited most of the major Marian shrines in the world. 'During my pilgrimages my visits to Marian sanctuaries have been, personally, the highest point with the people of God,' the Pope said upon landing at

Fatima, probably one of the most famous Marian shrines in the world. 'It is always with emotion, the same emotion, as the first time, that I place in the hands of Maria Santissima everything which I could have done or will ever do in the service of the holy church.' Such statements have brought the Pope tremendous popularity in Latin countries, where some prelates have recently disparaged veneration of Mary as a backward practice detracting from active social tasks. Marian devotion is said to have arisen in the East, where the Virgin is also revered by Islam. One of the Roman Catholic dogmas teaches that Mary conceived Christ without sexual intercourse, through divine intervention, and was assumed bodily into heaven. Pope Paul VI pictured her in a major 1974 document as the 'new woman' who took an active role in the early church and championed the rights of the weak against the powerful. But he criticized soft-hearted devotion, legendary elements and 'sterile and ephemeral sentimentality.' He deplored the profusion of 'Virgin appearances' around the world, branding it 'vain credulity and . . . the exaggerated search for novelties or extraordinary phenomena.' "

Pope John Paul II evidently does not have the inhibitions which characterized Paul VI. Mary is obviously the preeminent personage in the religious life of the current pope, and it seems that millions of people readily respond favorably to the modern Mariolatry! Such Mariolatry, however, has its roots deep in the past history and teaching of the Roman Catholic Church. Just as Paul courageously preached the gospel in spite of the pagan preeminence of Diana of Ephesus, so must gospel preachers today fearlessly proclaim the Lordship of Christ over all idolatry, religion and materialism.

A Perverted Adoration of Mary

Years ago Dr. Robert T. Ketcham wrote a review of the book *The Glories of Mary* by St. Alphonsus Ligouri. The review was made up largely of quotations from the book, but Dr. Ketcham prefaced the quotations with the following statement: "The Roman Catholic Church teaches that Mary is not only to be worshipped, but that she is our Savior. This book before me has seven hundred and ten pages. At least half of the book is dedicated to the proposition that no one can be saved except through Mary. It is pointed out that it is Christ's death which saves us, but that no sinner anywhere can reach the benefit of that death unless he appeals for it through Mary. She alone is the dispenser of the grace that comes from Christ to a sinner." Following are a few quotations from "Saint" Ligouri: "If God is angry with a sinner, and Mary takes him under her protection, she withholds the avenging arm of her Son and saves him" (p. 124); "That which we intend to prove here is, that the intercession of Mary is even necessary to salvation" (p. 154); When discussing Jesus' statement to John while Jesus was on the cross, in which Jesus said, "Behold thy mother," Ligouri wrote: "It is the same thing as if He (Jesus) had said: 'As no one can be saved except through the merits of my sufferings and death, so no one will be a partaker of the blood then shed otherwise than through the prayer of my Mother. My wounds are ever flowing fountains of grace; but their streams will reach no one but by the channel of Mary. In vain will he invoke me as a Father who has not venerated Mary as a Mother' " (p. 155); "All graces that have ever been bestowed on men, all came through Mary" (p. 159); "It must now be evident to all . . . that all graces that have been, that are, and will be dispensed to men to the end of the world through the merits of Christ, should be dispensed by the hands and through the intercession of Mary" (p. 162); "The way of salvation is open to none otherwise than through Mary" (p. 169); "Whoever asks and expects to obtain grace without the intercession of Mary, endeavors to fly without wings" (p. 162); "He who is protected by Mary will be saved; he who is not will be lost" (p. 170). "Whereas of all other virgins, we must say that they follow the Lamb whithersoever he goeth; of the blessed Virgin Mary we can say that the Lamb followed her" (p. 179); "At the command of Mary, all obey, even God" (p. 181); "Since the devil is the head of original sin, this head it was that Mary crushed" (p. 290); "How can she be otherwise than full of grace, who has made the ladder to paradise, the gate of heaven, the most true mediatress between God and man" (p. 153); "No one comes to me unless my Mother first of all draws him by her prayers" (p. 167); "There is no one, O most holy Mary, who can know God but through thee; no one can be delivered from dangers but through thee, O Virgin Mother; no one who obtains mercy but through thee, O filled with all grace" (p. 171); "For thy protection is omnipotent, O Mary" (p. 181). Lest you think Saint Ligouri speaks just for himself, the Roman Catholic publisher introduced *The Glories of Mary* with these words: "Everything that our saint has written is, as it were, a summary of a Catholic tradition on the subject that he treats: it is not an individual author; it is, so to speak, the Church herself that speaks to us." And, we might add, the "Church" speaks perverted adoration of Mary. Surely Mary herself would be ashamed of Ligouri's book.

Dr. Henry M. Woods has well written: "Mariolatry grew and became common, only as the Word of God was neglected, and apostasy spread through the Church. From the number of churches dedicated to the Virgin Mary in Rome, she would seem to be honored more than God or the Savior. Out of more than 400 churches and chapels in the city, only 5 are dedicated to the Holy Trinity, 15 to Christ, 2 to the Holy Spirit and 121 to the Virgin Mary! Moreover the Raccolta shows that language used in prayer to Mary is identical with that used to God" (Henry M. Woods, *Our Priceless Heritage, A Study of Christian Doctrine in Contrast with Romanism* [Harrisburg: Evangelical Press, 1953], p. 41). Dr. Woods has said what we Baptists need to repeat fearlessly from our pulpits: "The excuses which the Church of Rome makes to evade her guilt of the sin of idolatry are the very same that the heathen offer for their worship of idols. God's prohibition applies to every form of idolatry, whether to the idol worship of Hinduism or that of Rome: the image of St. Peter or of Mary is just as truly an idol as any idol of Buddhism and at the Judgment Day God will hold the leaders of the Roman Church responsible for deceiving the people and leading them into apostasy" (p. 44). Preaching against the idolatry of Romanism is necessary if we believe what Dr. John E. Dahlin wrote in the January-March 1980 edition of *The Discerner*, p. 5: "Mariology is fixed within the Catholic system. In fact, the veneration of Mary has increased and not diminished." (*The Discerner* is an interdenominational heresy-exposing quarterly published by Religion Analysis Service, Inc., P.O. Box 806, Brainerd, MN

56401-0806; 800-562-9153).

In his definitive work, Loraine Boettner gives us some helpful information about Mariolatry. "The devotions to Mary are undoubtedly the most spontaneous of any in the Roman Catholic worship. Attendance at Sunday mass is obligatory, under penalty of mortal sin if one is absent without a good reason, and much of the regular service is formalistic and routine. But the people by the thousands voluntarily attend novenas for the 'Sorrowful Mother.' Almost every religious order dedicates itself to the Virgin Mary. National shrines, such as those at Lourdes in France, Fatima in Portugal, Our Lady of Guadalupe in Mexico, are dedicated to her and attract millions. The Shrine of Anne de Beaupre, in Quebec, the most popular shrine in Canada, is dedicated to Saint Anne, who according to apocryphal literature was the mother of Mary. Thousands of churches, schools, hospitals, convents and shrines are dedicated to her glory. It is difficult for Protestants to realize the deep love and reverence that devout Roman Catholics have for the Virgin Mary. One must be immersed in and saturated with the Roman Catholic mind in order to feel its heartbeat. Says Margaret Shepherd, an ex nun: 'No words can define to my readers the feeling of reverential love I had for the Virgin Mary. As the humble suppliant kneels before her statue he thinks of her as the tender, compassionate mother of Jesus, the friend and mediatrix of sinners. The thought of praying to Christ for any special grace without seeking the intercession of Mary never occurred to me' (*My Life in the Convent*, p. 31). The titles given Mary are in themselves a revelation of Roman Catholic sentiment toward her. She is called: Mother of God, Queen of the Apostles, Queen of Heaven, Queen of the Angels, the Door of Paradise, the Gate of Heaven, Our Life, Mother of Grace, Mother of Mercy, and many others which ascribe to her supernatural powers" (Loraine Boettner, *Roman Catholicism* [Philadelphia: The Presbyterian and Reformed Publishing Co.] pp. 141, 142).

Loraine Boettner further writes: "The Church of Rome, without any warrant whatever from Scripture, technically divides worship into three kinds: (1) **Latria,** the supreme worship, given to God alone; (2) **Dulia,** a secondary kind of veneration given to saints and angels; and (3) **Hyperdulia,** a higher kind of veneration given to the Virgin Mary. The theory, however, is useless in practice, for the average worshipper is not able to make the distinctions, nor does he even know that such distinctions exist . . . We must insist that any religious worship, whether inward or outward, consisting of prayer, or praise, and expressed by outward homage such as bowing, kneeling, or prostration, is properly termed worship and belongs to God alone" (Boettner, pp. 150, 151). How we need to evangelize the dear people ensnared in the wily webs of Mariolatry!

A Proper Appraisal of Mary

The Word of God does properly honor Mary, even as the man Moses in the Old Testament and the apostle Paul in the New Testament are properly honored. Luke 1:28: "And the angel came in unto her, and said, Hail, thou that art highly favoured, the Lord is with thee: blessed art thou among women." Mary was a virtuous, valorous woman. But at no time did Mary usurp a place of eminence. She never described herself with titles of pomp or might. Rather, Mary exalted God. She said, "My soul doth magnify the Lord, and my spirit hath rejoiced in God MY SAVIOR" (Luke 1:46, 47). Mary recognized her own sinfulness and her need for a Savior. There is absolutely no Scriptural authority whatsoever for the Roman Catholic teachings of the Immaculate Conception as proclaimed by Pius IX in 1854 and the Bodily Assumption of Mary into Heaven as proclaimed by Pope Pius XII in 1950. Neither does the Bible give credence to the proclamation of Pope Paul VI in 1965 declaring Mary to be Mother of the Church. We may properly believe from Scriptural teaching that Mary bore other children after the supernatural birth of Jesus (Matt. 13:55); she ultimately died a natural death, was buried and now awaits the resurrection. The mention of her in Acts 1:14 indicates no special status: "These all continued with one accord in prayer and supplication, with the women, and Mary the mother of Jesus, and with his brethren."

One of the most delightful little books in my library is *The*

Mother of Jesus, Her Problems and Her Glory by A. T. Robertson, published by Baker Book House. The great New Testament scholar wrote: "As Christianity has made its way over the earth, the fame of Mary has grown. This was inevitable. Her life was literally wrapt up in the work of her Son. She was the greatest of mothers. She was the mother of the greatest of men, one called the Son of Man, but she was more. In some way still incomprehensible to us, as to her, she was the mother of the Son of God. The double mystery still baffles us, though our very reason compels acceptance and faith. Mary would not have us give her credit for aught save that she did her part well. The goodness and grace of God chose her as the channel for this mercy to the human race. So she occupies the highest pedestal among mothers, and mothers rank above all other persons. But this is not to place her above mortals because of the deity of her wondrous Son. She has her consolation in high duty nobly done and in the supreme character and service of her Son. That is her coronation. She needs no other . . . But, if Roman Catholics have deified Mary, Protestants, as a rule, have neglected her. This is largely due to a reaction against the adoration by the Catholics. Protestants have often been afraid to praise and esteem Mary for her full worth lest they be accused of leanings in sympathy with the Catholics. Hence it has come to pass that the noblest of mothers is still the most misunderstood of mothers and of women. Cold neglect on the one hand is hers while adoring worship greets her memory in countless statues on the other hand. The god whom multitudes worship today is Mary. Protestants fight Mariolatry in order to stand up for the worship of Mary's Son, our Savior" (pp. 66, 69). Preacher, do you feel a desire to prepare and preach two or three Biblical messages on Mary, perhaps during the Christmas season? I hope so. Present the positive, Biblical message of Mary. Lovingly but clearly expose the error of Mariolatry.

Since we firmly believe Mariolatry is one of the most serious challenges to Biblical Christianity in today's world, we urge our readers to combat it. To help you in your understanding of the twentieth century menace of Pope John Paul's brand of Roman doctrine, Dr. John Edward Millheim, Vice

President and Director of Baptist Bible School of Theology of Clarks Summit, Pennsylvania has updated and rewritten GARBC Literature Item 13 entitled *The Ecumenical Movement and the Roman Catholic Church.*

Let us pray that the General Association of Regular Baptist Churches will be spared the debilitating, internecine bickering and backbiting that has so weakened other groups of fundamentalists through the years. Let us turn the full force of our polemic powers upon the real enemies of our faith, the Mariolaters, the Mormons, the Moslems and the Modernists, the materialists and all other purveyors of anti-Christian philosophy. Let us work mightily in the power of the Spirit to bring more local churches into our Fellowship. In short, let us earnestly contend for the faith once delivered to the saints. Amen!

13

The Hole and the Hewing—
Our Heritage

The Hole

We are told to look unto "the hole of the pit whence ye are digged." The key word in this phrase is *pit*. The Hebrew word is *bore* or *bowr*. The word has to do with a pit hole, a cistern or a prison dungeon.

Two other references throw a great deal of light on the meaning of the pit hole spoken of here in Isaiah. Our reference is to Joseph in his traumatic experience with his jealous brothers. The Bible tells us: ". . . And Joseph went after his brethren, and found them in Dothan. And when they saw him afar off, even before he came near unto them, they conspired against him to slay him. And they said one to another, Behold, this dreamer cometh. Come now therefore, and let us slay him, and cast him into some pit, and we will say, Some evil beast hath devoured him: and we shall see what will become of his dreams" (Gen. 37:17–20). A pit can be a prison!

Then look at Psalm 40:1, 2, where David declares: "I waited patiently for the LORD; and he inclined unto me, and heard my cry. He brought me up also out of an horrible pit, out of the miry clay, and set my feet upon a rock, and established my goings."

Regular Baptists, look! Look unto the hole of the pit whence ye are digged. Meditate with joy on the prison from which you have been liberated, the horrible pit from which you have been lifted, the dungeon from which you have been delivered. Let me suggest two horrible holes from which we have been saved.

First, the pit hole of *degradation*. Charles H. Gabriel exclaimed and my redeemed heart sings: "From sinking sand He lifted me, with tender hand He lifted me; from shades of night to plains of light, O, praise His name, He lifted me!" Regular Baptists are redeemed Baptists. We've been washed in the blood, emancipated from the Evil One, set free from the prison house of sin. The foul fetters have been broken, the chains have been shattered, and we shout with Charles Wesley: "Long my imprisoned spirit lay fast bound in sin and nature's night. Thine eye diffused a quick-'ning ray: I woke—the dungeon flamed with light! My chains fell off, my heart was free! I rose, went forth, and followed Thee." Thank God, we've been lifted from the pit hole of degradation.

Second, the pit hole of *denominationalism*. Sixty years ago, Bible-believing Baptists in the Northern Baptist Convention were embroiled in a controversy that would wax hotter and hotter until the only thing left to obedient believers was clear-cut separation from the Convention.

The pit of denominationalism had three characteristics that vexed the souls of all Regular Baptists. The Convention was characterized by *infidelity in pronouncements*. Two examples will suffice here. Harry Emerson Fosdick was fond of saying, "Of course I do not believe in the virgin birth, or in that old-fashioned substitutionary doctrine of the atonement, and I do not know any intelligent person who does." Thank God we are delivered from that kind of a doctrinal dungeon! Regular Baptists repudiated Fosdick's infidelity and we continue to proclaim the precious doctrines of Christ's virgin birth and the substitutionary atonement. Another example of infidelity in pronouncements is the blasphemous statement of Nels Ferre, for years a faculty member of the apostate Andover-Newton Baptist Theological Seminary. He said, "To call Jesus God is to substitute an idol for incarnation." In 1932, Regular Baptists were delivered from such denominational unbelief.

The Convention was also characterized by *inclusivism in policy*. The Convention's Foreign Mission Board in the 1920s was sending Bible-believing missionaries out to work on mission fields alongside outright modernists. The Convention's Home Mission Society appointed a man to be superintendent of the Boston Baptist City Mission just hours after he had said, "The blood of Jesus Christ is of no more value in the salvation of a soul than the water in which Pilate washed his hands." This is the hole of the pit from which Regular Baptists were dug some fifty years ago. The Convention's inclusivist policy permitted pastors, missionaries and seminary professors to be part of the denominational program while denying the fundamentals of the faith. Such a hole could not be tolerated by true Baptists.

The Convention was also characterized by *imperialism in practice*. Denominational dictatorship and interference in local church matters were hallmarks of the convention in the 1920s. Many years ago Dr. Robert T. Ketcham wrote: "We charge, and the charges can be sustained by incidents across the whole length and breadth of the American Baptist Convention, that denominational secretaries use their influence to keep good men out of Baptist pulpits, that they use their influence to put modernistic men into pulpits, and now in addition to that we maintain that secretaries and denominational officials, upon occasion, have been known to deliberately practice and advocate deception in the matter of placing modernists in fundamental pulpits." What a pit of perversion and ecclesiastical evil we have been saved from! Praise the Lord for His grace and mercy to us.

The Hewing

Our text directs us to "look unto the rock whence ye are hewn." God has been wonderfully at work during these past fifty years carving, chiseling, cutting and shaping the "rock" known as the General Association of Regular Baptist Churches. It is a hallowed, wholesome hewing that we look back upon with deep gratitude and amazement. With John Newton we can exclaim: "Thro' many dangers, toils and snares I have already come; 'tis grace that brought me safe thus far, and grace will lead me home."

Both Old and New Testament writers have often referred

to rocks and stones in their descriptions of the believer's relationship to God. Our Lord said: "Therefore whosoever heareth these sayings of mine, and doeth them, I will liken him unto a wise man, which built his house upon a rock" (Matt. 7:24). Concerning Peter's testimony, "Thou art the Christ, the Son of the living God," Jesus said, ". . . upon this rock I will build my church; and the gates of hell shall not prevail against it" (Matt. 16:16-18). The apostle Paul wrote: "According to the grace of God which is given unto me, as a wise masterbuilder, I have laid the foundation, and another buildeth thereon. But let every man take heed how he buildeth thereupon. For other foundation can no man lay than that is laid, which is Jesus Christ" (1 Cor. 3:10, 11). The New International Version translates 1 Peter 2:4 and 5 beautifully with these words: "As you come to him, the living Stone—rejected by men but chosen by God and precious to him—you also, like living stones, are being built into a spiritual house to be a holy priesthood, offering spiritual sacrifices acceptable to God through Jesus Christ."

The "hewing out" of the GARBC has been accomplished with three major tools. First, *separation from apostasy.* We believe and obey 2 John 9-11: "Whosoever transgresseth, and abideth not in the doctrine of Christ, hath not God. He that abideth in the doctrine of Christ, he hath both the Father and the Son. If there come any unto you, and bring not this doctrine, receive him not into your house, neither bid him God speed: For he that biddeth him God speed is partaker of his evil deeds." We believe and obey 2 Corinthians 6:14-18, which is translated superbly in the New American Standard Bible with these words: "Do not be bound together with unbelievers: for what partnership have righteousness and lawlessness, or what fellowship has light with darkness? Or what harmony has Christ with Belial, or what has a believer in common with an unbeliever? Or what agreement has the temple of God with idols? For we are the temple of the living God; just as God said, 'I will dwell in them and walk among them; and I will be their God, and they shall be My people. Therefore, come out from their midst and be separate, says the Lord. And do not touch what is unclean; and I will welcome you. And I will be a father to you, and you shall be sons and daughters to Me, says the Lord Almighty.' "

Our separation from the apostasy of the 1932 Northern Baptist Convention was in full obedience to these passages written by John and Paul. We remain to this day wholly separated from the apostasy.

The second major tool used by God in the "hewing out" of the GARBC may be described as *sensitivity to autonomy*. Regular Baptists are *independent* Baptists. Written into Article XIV of our GARBC Articles of Faith are these key words: ". . . We hold that the local church has the absolute right of self-government free from the interference of any hierarchy of individuals or organizations." Our sensitivity to autonomy has given our Association of local churches a unique relationship with Baptist educational, missionary and benevolent agencies. Article VII of our Constitution says: "It shall be the policy of the Association to abstain from the creation and/or control of educational, missionary and other benevolent agencies."

Many outsiders do not understand the importance of this mutual autonomy enjoyed by our churches and agencies. We came out of the Northern Baptist Convention where denominational control of colleges, seminaries, mission boards and benevolent agencies was taken for granted. Our Association has been organized to avoid such denominationalism. We own no schools. We own no mission boards. We own no social agencies. We control none. And we in no way coerce our local churches to financially support them. What our churches do, they do voluntarily. Our agencies are, therefore, as independent as our churches. Agencies are only approved as worthy of our support, but no local church is obligated to agree with the Association's majority vote to approve.

Dr. Joseph Stowell once said, "Our churches are as independent as hogs on ice!" But such autonomy is healthy when it is disciplined by a desire to further the work of Christ with others of like precious faith. The advantages that may characterize denominational uniformity and centralization may appeal to less adventuresome people, but Regular Baptists prefer the liberty of our autonomy and the diversity of our independence. We are not isolated churches. We are truly independent, but we are also interdependent. Since our Associational work is interwoven with our twenty approved agencies on a voluntary basis, there is an unusual strength and resiliency to our whole movement. Our soundness of doctrine gives us a strength in diversity of operation that is truly unique in Christendom.

The third major tool used by our Lord in the "hewing" process I call *service as ambassadors*. We are people with a proclamation, men with a message. Missionary evangelism has characterized our movement from its beginnings. The winning of converts, the discipling of believers, the planting of churches at home and around the world have always occupied our brains, our brawn, our billfolds and our heartbeats. The gospel of salvation through the finished work of Christ has never been exchanged by Regular Baptists for a social gospel based on political or moral reformation. The Great Commission is a clarion battle cry sending our people to the four corners of the earth to preach the gospel. We are Heaven's ambassadors, not Washington's social workers. Evangelization, not economics or environmentalism, is our thrust.

Dr. Charles U. Wagner has poetically captured the world's wretchedness and the believer's responsibility in these words:

> In darkened jungles, heathen tribes
>   Through ritual's rite do pray and strive;
> Salvation's plan has ne'er been told
>   For no man careth for their souls.
>
> In darkened mazes and distant places,
>   Lost among neglected races;
> A desperate cry, now faint and low,
>   "No man careth for my soul."
>
> In college campus confusion
>   And intellectual delusion;
> Bombastic causes—harsh and bold,
>   But no man careth for their souls.
>
> In cloistered confines of the home
>   An alcoholic wife—alone;
> So sick of habit's terrible toll,
>   And no man careth for her soul.

> In churches fine and formal crowds,
>   With lofty steeples high and proud;
> With proper people, kind but cold,
>   But no man careth for my soul.
>
> At home, abroad, the burdened sigh,
>   The empty heart, the desperate cry;
> O, Christian, give; O, Christian, go;
>   O Christian, care, care for their souls.

For more than 60 years Regular Baptists have given, gone and cared for souls. An Association of evangelistic, missionary-supporting local churches has been "hewn out" of the "rock" of 2 Corinthians 5:20: "Now then we are ambassadors for Christ, as though God did beseech you by us: we pray you in Christ's stead, be ye reconciled to God."

Frightful the hole from which we were dug! Faithful the hewing to make us what we are! Now let's look at the rest of the text from Isaiah 51:1.

The Hearkening

"Hearken to me, ye that follow after righteousness, ye that seek the LORD." Surely as we move ahead in the will of God, we must be concerned with following after righteousness. To hearken to righteousness is to seek the Lord and His will. To hearken is to be obedient to His Word. As an Association, I believe we need to hearken to a righteous concentration, a righteous cause and a righteous charity.

First, *a righteous concentration.* God's people are constantly being tempted to tangents and diverted to detours. How we need to hearken to Samuel's words spoken to Israel in 1 Samuel 12:21: "And turn ye not aside: for then should ye go after vain things, which cannot profit nor deliver; for they are vain." Fundamentalists are not immune to tangents. Fundamental Baptists are not immune to dangerous detours. There is a great need today for a Biblically balanced, Scripturally sage, spiritual statesmanship in fundamentalist circles. Fundamentalism needs the General Association of Regular Baptist Churches as never before. For half a century now we have refused to allow ourselves to be drawn away by peripheral issues that dissipate our energies, dilute our effectiveness and detour our evangelistic efforts. We must know what the issue of the day is if we are to stand where we ought to stand, and I want to be as forthright and helpful about that keynote matter as possible.

The issue is *not* which version of the Bible is the best. *The issue* in Christendom today is the inerrancy of *the Bible* as originally written. The battle is *not* over translations, *not* over the virtues of versions; *the battle,* as Harold Lindsell's book so correctly put it, is for *the Bible* itself. The integrity of the Bible demands its inerrancy. The infallibility of the Bible demands its inerrancy. The verbal, plenary inspiration of the Bible demands its inerrancy. Failure to hold to the inerrancy of the Bible has ruined once-great denominations. The Southern Baptist Convention is right now in a life-and-death struggle over this very issue. The GARBC has been called to the kingdom for such a time as this! Let us not allow ourselves to be diverted to a debate over the versions. Let us not at this critical hour in our history allow ourselves to be taken off on a translations tangent. Let us see the issue clearly.

As English-speaking Regular Baptists, we stand unashamedly, unabashedly and unwaveringly for the inerrancy of the Word of God. Our GARBC statement of faith declares: "We believe in the authority and sufficiency of the Holy Bible, consisting of the sixty-six books of the Old and New Testaments, as originally written; that it was verbally and plenarily inspired and is the product of Spirit-controlled men, and therefore is infallible and inerrant in all matters of which it speaks."

Think of the original manuscripts of the Word of God as a majestic, literary Mount Everest towering over all the great literary hills and mountains of man's genius. That infallible, inerrant mountain of God-breathed Scriptures has challenged the greatest minds of consecrated scholarship through the centuries. The sanctified summits of the holy Hebrew and glorious Greek have been prayerfully and meticulously scaled by translators from generation to generation. Lofty Latin, gruff German, fair French, baffling Bengali, proud Portuguese, suave Spanish, challenging Chinese, enterprising English—all these and hundreds of other tongues and dialects have been pressed into the tedious, tantalizing, treasured toil of translating the magnificent Word of God into the various vernaculars of the peoples of the earth. We humbly and happily salute those triumphant translators today.

We salute John Wycliffe, who is called "The Morning Star of the Reformation." We salute William Tyndale, whose translation in many ways was the forerunner of the King James Version, which came seventy-five years after Tyndale's martyrdom. We salute Miles Coverdale, who gave the English-speaking world its first completed Bible in print. We thank God for those noble men who labored long on the challenging crags and crevices and cliffs of the Scriptural Mount Everest. Our gratitude is boundless for that marvelous team of translators who gave us the King James Version.

Now let me express my gratitude for sanctified scholars of the twentieth century who also long to accurately and authoritatively translate the Word of God into the language of today's English-speaking world. Let us not belittle or bemean their legitimate and learned efforts. Thank God for the "mountain climbers," those tenacious translators who gave us the American Standard Version of 1901. Thank God for those Bible-loving men who carefully and prayerfully endeavored to translate the Word of God into our vernacular and thus gave us the New American Standard Bible of 1960. Thank God for the vitality and vision, not unlike that of the seventeenth-century King James team, who have given us the New International Version. "Mount Everest" continues to challenge the greatest linguists. The "mountain" of Holy Writ continues to occupy consecrated editors and writers in giving to the world admirable and authentic versions of the incomparably inspired, inexhaustibly inerrant and infinitely infallible Word of God.

While we rightly stand guard against new evangelicals, we must also be alert to the perils of new fundamentalists who would seek to create new tests for fellowship among true fundamentalists—tests that never before have been permitted to divide and splinter the ranks of historical fundamentalists.

The General Association of Regular Baptist Churches

must recognize that it is *not* our responsibility to be arguing over different versions. Our holy task is to proclaim that the Bible itself is the Word of God. Pastors and professors, as veritable field commanders in what Lindsell called *The Battle for the Bible,* must be absolutely convinced that the fortress of our faith is the Word of God as originally and inerrantly given by God. One Regular Baptist may prefer a 1611 translation or version. Another Regular Baptist may prefer a 1901 version. Still another will choose the 1978 New International Version. But all must agree the versions have as the bedrock upon which they rest original manuscripts that were inerrantly given by God Himself. "For ever, O LORD, thy word is settled in heaven" (Ps. 119:89). This is the central issue of our day, *the inerrancy of the Word of God,* and on this vital Article of Faith the GARBC stands unflinchingly, inflexibly and unfailingly.

Thank God for the men in 1611 who produced a new translation. We bless God for what their work has meant to the English-speaking world for the past 370 years. Now, let's not fail to respect the courageous Christian scholars of the twentieth century who would as sincerely and as correctly seek to give us the Bible in as readable and accurate a translation as possible. Let's rally around the great cardinal doctrine of the verbal, plenary inspiration of the Word of God. Let's hold high the banner of the inerrancy of God-breathed Scripture. But let's cease and desist from any effort to make any one translation or version a test of fellowship or fundamentalism.

In addition to hearkening to a righteous concentration on the key issue of the day, we need to hearken to *a righteous cause.* That righteous cause is the planting of New Testament churches throughout the length and breadth of our land and the countries of the world. Are you aware there are 2,591 towns and cities in the United States with over 10,000 in population? Hundreds upon hundreds of these population centers need a Regular Baptist church. Oh, that God would raise up a mighty army of men to meet this challenge.

Did you know there are 207 metropolitan areas in the world with more than 500,000 population each? Of these great metropolitan areas, 163 number more than 1 million people. Who will tell these masses of humanity the gospel message?

Who will reach a lost and dying world of 4 billion, 600 million people? That is our righteous cause. Presently about 2,000 missionaries are in the ranks of our approved missionary agencies. They are working on 60 foreign fields and the home field. How we need to hearken to our Lord's command in Matthew 9:38, "Pray ye therefore the Lord of the harvest, that he will send forth labourers into his harvest."

We also need to hearken to a *righteous charity*. Look closely at the exhortations in 1 Corinthians 16:13, 14: "Watch ye, stand fast in the faith, quit you like men, be strong. Let all your things be done with charity." Regular Baptists must watch; we must be characterized by *vigilance*. We must stand fast in the faith; we must be marked by *veracity*. We must quit like men, we must be distinguished by *valor*. We must be strong; we must be known by *vigor*. But notice: "Let all your things be done with charity." We must in all of our vigilance, veracity, valor and vigor be characterized by the supreme *virtue*, the love of God.

The General Association of Regular Baptist Churches is a Fellowship. We are blood-bought brothers and sisters in Christ. We've been delivered from the hole of denominationalism that was characterized by deceit, suspicion, political machinations and doctrinal infidelity. God has graciously hewn us out a fellowship of churches in which we have freedom to preach the blessed Biblical doctrines we hold dear. We have banded together because we are Regular Baptists and Biblical separatists. We may not always agree with each other on non-doctrinal matters, but we are agreed on the great truths stated in our Articles of Faith. On these Biblical doctrines and Baptist distinctives we are inflexible.

We are also agreed that Regular Baptists are not to be regimented by any hierarchy of individuals or councils. Christian charity demands that we know the difference between principles and preferences. Such discernment will enable us to work together even though we have some diversities and differences among us. Such Regular Baptist New Testament freedom surely beats denominational rigidity and Convention-controlled conformity.

An Association that exercises such righteous charity will

grow and glow. We'll have something to offer to those in the north and south who are sick of Convention inability to deal with unbelief in high places. Let's hold out the hand of help to them. Let's tell them about a GARBC that's happy to be out of the hole, grateful for what God has hewn out, and faithful to the blessed work of hearkening unto the Lord.

14

Marriage and Divorce

WITHOUT A doubt, one of the tragic trends in the United States of America is the popularity of easy divorce. The United States Census Bureau tells us there was one divorce for every seven marriages in the U.S.A. in 1920. In 1940, one divorce for every six marriages. In 1960, one divorce for every four marriages. In 1972, one divorce for every three marriages. In 1978, one divorce for every two and one-half marriages. Nineteen seventy-eight also marked a menacing milestone: there were one million divorces recorded in that year. Nineteen seventy-nine was worse. Think of it! One million broken homes per year in the U.S.A.! Divorce is a curse and a scourge. The disintegration of marriages, the degradation of divorce and the consequent moral complications of remarriages have become the most knotty problems facing twentieth-century pastors. I have studied the Word of God prayerfully and carefully with reference to this whole problem, and the following comments comprise a Biblical viewpoint which will, I trust, give you answers that are adequate as you face people who have been torn by this traumatic divorce devastation. Pastors, of all people, should look to the Bible for their answers. Humanistic sociologists cannot and must not be the ones to formulate our responses to marital difficulties; only the Word of God gives the authoritative answers needed by people whose lives have been shattered and broken.

The Creation of Sexuality

"And it came to pass, that when Jesus had finished these

sayings, he departed from Galilee, and came into the coasts of Judaea beyond Jordan; And great multitudes followed him; and he healed them there. The Pharisees also came unto him, tempting him, and saying unto him, Is it lawful for a man to put away his wife for every cause? And he answered and said unto them, Have ye not read, that he which made them at the beginning made them male and female, And said, For this cause shall a man leave father and mother, and shall cleave to his wife: and they two shall be one flesh? Wherefore they are no more twain, but one flesh. What therefore God hath joined together, let not man put asunder. They say unto him, Why did Moses then command to give a writing of divorcement, and to put her away? He saith unto them, Moses because of the hardness of your hearts suffered you to put away your wives: but from the beginning it was not so. And I say unto you, Whosoever shall put away his wife, except it be for fornication, and shall marry another, committeth adultery: and whoso marrieth her which is put away doth commit adultery. His disciples say unto him, If the case of the man be so with his wife, it is not good to marry. But he said unto them, All men cannot receive this saying, save they to whom it is given. For there are some eunuchs, which were so born from their mother's womb: and there are some eunuchs, which were made eunuchs of men: and there be eunuchs, which have made themselves eunuchs for the kingdom of heaven's sake. He that is able to receive it, let him receive it" (Matt. 19:1–12).

I have given the above space to this passage because I believe it is the crucial portion of God's Word with reference to the divorce–remarriage issue. The passage makes it clear that the maker of sexuality is God. When a person debases sexuality, that person is guilty of degrading what God has created for our blessing. We must also note that the making is distinctive. Men are to relate sexually only to women. Women are to relate sexually only to men. The Maker is Deity, and the making is distinctive. He made them male and female. To anyone who is intellectually honest, our Lord's declaration simply means that homosexuality and lesbianism are sinful life-styles. No one is born a lesbian. No one is born a homosexual. They are learned life-styles. God's Word makes it clear that masculinity is to characterize males and femininity is to characterize females. God has so ordained sexuality.

The Constitution of Marriage

According to the Lord Jesus Christ, there are three things involved in the constituting of a marriage. We find them in Matthew 19:5. First, marriage requires **leaving.** "For this cause shall a man leave father and mother." We pastors must teach our young people that marriage means leaving one's parents in order to establish a new relationship and a new home. That is God's will. When the principle of leaving is violated, there is trouble. So-called in-law problems are the result of parents or their children or both failing to leave as the Bible commands. Children are to leave their parents. Parents are not to interfere with their married sons and daughters.

Second, marriage requires **cleaving.** Jesus said: "For this cause shall a man leave father and mother, and shall cleave to his wife." That word could be translated "adhere to." It has to do with glue. Pastors must teach young couples that men are to be cleavers. An Old Testament commentary on this cleaving principle is found in Proverbs 5:18, 19: "Let thy fountain be blessed: and rejoice with the wife of thy youth. Let her be as the loving hind and pleasant roe; let her breasts satisfy thee at all times; and be thou ravished always with her love."

Third, marriage involves **weaving.** Jesus said: "For this cause shall a man leave father and mother, and shall cleave to his wife: and the two shall be one flesh." Marriage means two people whose personalities, whose bodies, whose emotions, whose intellects, whose very spirits are woven into one another so that they wonderfully become one. The warp and woof of the tapestry of their lives becomes one. Notice that Jesus says "they two shall be one," not they three, not they five but they two shall be one. Note also that He speaks of one man plus one woman; not one man plus another man, or one woman plus another woman. The two shall be one. The Bible teaches monogamy, not polygamy. When men became polygamists in Old Testament times, they brought trauma, trial and tribulation into their family circles. The constitution of marriage requires, therefore, the **leaving** of home by one man in order for him to **cleave** to one woman in order to **weave** their lives into one marital tapestry which Jesus refers to as "one flesh."

The Condemnation of Divorce

Before we carefully look at the Biblical teaching on divorce, let us make it clear that pastors must always practice "speaking the truth in love" (Eph. 4:15). "And the servant of the Lord must not strive; but be gentle unto all men, apt to teach, patient, In meekness instructing those that oppose themselves; if God peradventure will give them repentance to the acknowledging of the truth; And that they may recover themselves out of the snare of the devil, who are taken captive by him at his will" (2 Tim. 2:24-26). We must teach what the Bible has to say on the subject of divorce compassionately, courageously and clearly to bring our people to the acknowledging of the truth. Divorce is a snare of the devil from which we must rescue our people. We are not concerned with what the law allows, or with what some denomination allows, or with what some psychologist teaches, but what the Bible says is the will of God with reference to marriage, divorce and remarriage. That is the information and instruction we must know.

First, let us consider the permanence of marriage. In Matthew 19:6, Jesus said: "What therefore God hath joined together, let not man put asunder." Without any doubt, Jesus taught the permanence of marriage. In Ephesians 5 we are told that marriage is a picture of the relationship between Christ and His Church, and we read these words: "For we are members of his body, of his flesh, and of his bones" (Eph. 5:30). The relationship between Christ and His Church is indissoluble. Our Lord affirmed that when He declared: "My sheep hear my voice, and I know them, and they follow me: And I give unto them eternal life; and they shall never perish, neither shall any man pluck them out of my hand" (John 10:27-29). Jesus is there teaching eternal security. In Ephesians 5 Paul is illustrating eternal security with the marriage relationship. Marriage is to be a permanent relationship. "For the woman which hath an husband is bound by the law to her husband so long as he liveth; but if the husband be dead, she is loosed from the law of her husband. So then if, while her husband liveth, she be married to another man, she shall be called an adulteress: but if her husband be dead, she is free from that law; so that she is no adulteress, though she be married to another man" (Rom. 7:2, 3).

Second, let us consider the prohibition of divorce. I want you to see this Biblical ban in both the Old and New Testaments. Jesus declares in Matthew 19 that from the beginning it was never God's will that people be divorced. The Jews had become very lax about the prohibition, and the Pharisees tried to get Jesus involved in a debate about Mosaic practices. Jesus absolutely ignored what they said about Moses; He also ignored what they said about divorce for every cause; and He took them right back to the very beginning and made it plain that God has in His will no provision for divorce.

The Old Testament closes with the prophet making the following point: "Therefore take heed to your spirit, and let none deal treacherously against the wife of his youth. For the LORD, the God of Israel, saith that he hateth putting away" (Mal. 2:15, 16). What was true at the close of the Old Testament era was many more times true at the beginning of the New Testament era, and Jesus was flying right in the face of the same problem we have in the U.S.A. today, easy divorce. Prevalent divorce. Malachi faced that problem. Jesus faced that problem. We face that problem. Do we cave in to it? Do we say, "It's too entrenched to fight it"? Malachi said, "God hates divorce!" He did not say God hates divorcees. Neither should we. But we must preach and teach the Biblical prohibition against divorce. We must stem the tide. We must establish godly standards for spouses and Biblical morals for marriages.

Now let us look at the New Testament. Mark 10:11, 12: "Whosoever shall put away his wife, and marry another, committeth adultery against her. And if a woman shall put away her husband, and be married to another, she committeth adultery." Luke 16:18: "Whosoever putteth away his wife, and marrieth another, committeth adultery: and whosoever marrieth her that is put away from her husband committeth adultery." First Corinthians 7:39: "The wife is bound by the law as long as her husband liveth; but if her husband be dead, she is at liberty to be married to whom she will; only in the Lord." We have already looked at Romans 7:2, 3. All of these passages teach clearly the prohibition of divorce.

Third, let us consider the purpose of Matthew 19:9: "Whosoever shall put away his wife, except it be for fornication, and shall marry another, committeth adultery: and whoso marrieth her which is put away doth commit adultery." With reference to this statement, I want to give you an explanation, an example and an exhortation.

The explanation. One major, basic rule of Bible interpretation which must not be violated, if one is to understand Scripture, is to always get the teaching of every clear passage on a subject and insist that any vague passage be interpreted so that it is consistent with all the clear passages. It is clear throughout the Bible that God hates divorce. All of the New Testament passages we have considered prohibit divorce and subsequent remarriage. There is one book which seems to contradict Mark, Luke, Romans and First Corinthians. That book is Matthew. The chapter is 19 and the verse is 9. This verse must fit into the rest of the Bible consistently, and it can! We must find out what Jesus is talking about when He says "except" and in doing so we will have the explanation. The Gospel of Matthew was written with the Jew in mind. In the Gospel of Mark, Jesus flatly says that divorce and remarriage constitute adultery. He says nothing about exception in Mark or Luke or Romans or Corinthians. Why? Because those books were written to Gentiles. Why is that important to note?

It is important and crucial because Jesus was in the Matthew setting, talking to a Jewish audience about a Jewish practice known as betrothal. In the Jewish culture, when a young man wanted to marry a girl, the parents got together and decided when they should become man and wife. At a ceremony where money was exchanged and a document was signed, a man and a woman were declared betrothed. As far as Jewish law was concerned, they were married even though the daughter would go back home with her parents and the son would return home with his parents. He would then spend about a year preparing for the actual public wedding. During that time of betrothal there would be no sexual contact, nothing. But in the eyes of the law that girl was married to that man just as if they had consummated that marital relationship by sexual intercourse. Now, because this was true, the Jews were very precise about their use of language. Fornication and adultery were two different sins in the Jewish culture. Adultery was a sin committed by a person whose marriage had been consummated. Adultery could not be committed by somebody who was simply betrothed. And the penalty for adultery was not putting away; it was stoning—death! So Jesus is not talking in Matthew 19:9 about adultery on the part of someone who is married. He it talking about fornication, sexual unfaithfulness on the part of someone who is betrothed or, as we would say, engaged. Therefore, if you want to paraphrase Matthew 19:9, we could read it as follows: "Except it be for fornication during the betrothal period." What Jesus teaches in Matthew is for the Jewish culture. No permission is granted by Him for divorce and remarriage. Such conduct is clearly defined by Him as adultery. If adultery and fornication were interchangeable terms, they would not both be listed when sins are categorized. But when sins are listed in Matthew 15:19 and Galatians 5:19, both adultery and fornication are listed. Adultery always refers to a sin committed by married people. Fornication always refers to a sin committed by single or betrothed people. Jesus is saying there can be no putting away of a woman except it be during the betrothal period. Before that man has ever sexually consummated his marriage to that woman, if she betrays him before actual marriage, then, and only then, does he have the right to put her away.

The example. Let me give you the clearest example in the Bible of what I have just explained. Matthew 1:18: "Now the birth of Jesus Christ was on this wise: When as his mother Mary was espoused to Joseph, before they came together, she was found with child of the Holy Ghost." Mary and Joseph were in that betrothal period. Joseph had signed the contract, made the agreement with Mary's parents and gone back home. Sometime during that betrothal period, Mary was found to be with child. And then notice what verse 19 says: "Then Joseph her husband, being a just man , and not willing to make her a publick example, was minded to put her away privily." That was his right! Joseph mistakenly thought Mary had betrayed him during the betrothal period. So did his neighbors, and they never accepted the account of the virgin birth. And what did the Jews call that sin? Or what they thought was sin? We have the answer in John 8:41: "Then said they to him, We be not born of fornication." Jesus lived all His life on earth with that nasty implication. They said fornication, not adultery. They meant: You are the son of a woman who betrayed her fiance. They were not saying: You are the son of a married woman who committed adultery. The exception clause appears only in Matthew because that book was written especially to the Jews. Mark was written to the Greeks. Luke was written to the Romans. No exception clause is found in those books. Clearly divorce is sin and the remarriage of divorced persons is compounded sin.

The exhortation. We must concentrate on making better marriages if we would successfully stem the tide of divorce in our churches. Pastors must adequately counsel with couples before marriage.

We must also lovingly counsel divorcees in our churches against remarriage. We must also be compassionate toward those who have already remarried; however, we should carefully teach them and all of our people what the Bible says with regard to divorce. Instead of giving in to the evil of divorce, we must concentrate on the Biblical education of our young people with reference to the permanent, sacred relationship of marriage.

Furthermore, we need to uphold Biblical standards of leadership in our churches. First Timothy 3:12 makes it clear that deacons are to be "the husbands of one wife." First Timothy 3:2 requires a pastor to be "the husband of one wife." He must be "blameless" or without reproach. Surely a man who has been guilty of marital infidelity disqualifies himself from the pastoral office. Paul instructed Timothy in a day when immorality, polygamy and easy divorce were rampant. Because we live in a similar world is no excuse for us to compromise Biblical standards. Let us in the GARBC compassionately, clearly and courageously lead our people to Biblical convictions about marriage and divorce.

15

A Great Door and Effectual Is Opened

THE APOSTLE Paul wrote words which are appropriate for Regular Baptists at this time in their history. I refer to 1 Corinthians 16:9: "For a great door and effectual is opened unto me, and there are many adversaries." The apostle's declaration immediately provokes some purposeful questions for the serious listener: *Who* opened the door? *What kind* of door has been opened? *Who* is trying to close the door and *why?*

For us as well as for Paul, *God* has opened the door. That door is described as *great* and *effectual*. It is the kind of opportunity that will display the greatness of our God and demand the best of our efforts. This door means a worldwide program and a wonder-working power. It is great and effectual. It is quantitative and qualitative. It is an opportunity which will demonstrate God's omnipotence, but it will also demand our obedience.

Paul also speaks of adversaries. The question automatically arises: Who is trying to close the door and why? Obviously, Satan wants the door closed. Regular Baptists are not unfamiliar with Satan's hatred of our Bible-centered, Christ-honoring program of worldwide evangelization and church-planting ministries. But the apostle speaks of *many* adversaries, and many there are. Space will not permit us to list all the atheistic, agnostic, liberal, neoorthodox, new evangelical and secular adversaries.

But, thank God, the door is open! Never before has the General Association of Regular Baptist Churches been more needed than right now. We have something the Bible-believing, independent Baptists of America need. We must begin anew to show them by our missionaries and by our manners that the GARBC is a great and effectual Fellowship with which to work and witness. We must know where we are going. Then others of like precious faith will want to go with us. In this day of drifting evangelicalism, drooling liberalism and drowsy fundamentalism, we must lead the way for God's people with the discerning, directive and dynamic New Testament Christianity which is the very warp and woof of GARBC theology and polity.

We have something to offer—an open door, an effectual door. We have Someone to obey, and He is greater than the adversaries, greater than the adversities, greater than the advocates of compromise and caution. The General Association of Regular Baptist Churches is worthy of something more than mere lip service. From a positive standpoint, we have what believers need today. From a negative viewpoint, we are opposed to a Christianity which is diluted by a compromising message, debilitated by a carnal morality or degraded by a charismatic mentality. I am concerned that we focus our attention on three major areas that are open and effectual arenas of activity for Regular Baptists.

Education Based on Biblical Inerrancy

Make no mistake about it, the Word of God is under vicious yet veiled attack today. The attack is viable because those who are speaking and writing against the inerrancy of Scripture are people who call themselves *friends* of the Bible. But let it be said by Regular Baptists that no one is a true friend of the Word of God who denies the Bible's historical authenticity, scientific accuracy and ethical authority. An infallibility without inerrancy is a contradictory camouflage which seeks to cover accommodations and concessions to pseudoscience and pseudointellectualism.

The psalmist declared: "I will worship toward thy holy temple, and praise thy name for thy lovingkindness and for thy truth: for thou hast magnified thy word above all thy name" (Ps. 138:2). Jesus declared most emphatically in John 10:35: "The scripture cannot be broken." He also said, "Think not that I am come to destroy the law, or the prophets: I am not come to destroy, but to fulfil. For verily I say unto you, Till heaven and earth pass, one jot or one tittle shall in no wise pass from the law, till all be fulfilled" (Matt. 5:17, 18). These and many other passages form the basis for the first paragraph of the GARBC articles of faith which declare our conviction that the Bible "is infallible and inerrant in all matters of which it speaks."

This belief in the inerrancy of Scripture must pervade and permeate every educational area of our Associational relationships. Our local chuches must be bastions of Biblical inerrancy. We must make certain that our Christian day schools are solidly built on the infallibility and inerrancy of the Bible. Our approved colleges and seminaries must wholeheartedly contend for this particular article of the faith. Not one teacher, administrator or board member must ever be tolerated on any of our campuses if that person has any reservations whatsoever about inerrancy.

We are an Association of *churches*. As such, we must set standards of educational excellence which reflect the true-to-the-Bible convictions of our local churches. We must preach the doctrine of Biblical inerrancy from our pulpits, teach it in our Sunday School classes and include it in our Christian day school instruction. We must encourage our colleges and seminaries to ceaselessly, relentlessly and faithfully reinforce the inerrancy conviction in the classroom, from the chapel platform and in the writings of its faculty members.

An education based on Biblical inerrancy demands a publishing arm like the Regular Baptist Press. Our Sunday School literature and every book and pamphlet published by RBP must continue to honor the Word of God. Our literature must educate and evangelize, but it must also warn and war. It must rectify if it is to edify.

Listen to the words of Hebrews 4:12: "For the word of God is quick, and powerful, and sharper than any two-edged sword, piercing even to the dividing asunder of soul and spirit, and of the joints and marrow, and is a discerner of the thoughts and intents of the heart." Brethren, if we have an infallible Book, and we do; if we have an inerrant Book, and we do; if we have a Book authored by the Holy Spirit Himself, and we do; if we have a Book that is forever settled in Heaven, and we do; if we have a Book that is a lamp unto our feet and a light unto our path, and we do; if we have a Book that is the Sword of the Spirit, and we do; *let us preach it!* Paul thundered: "Preach the word" (2 Tim. 4:2). Let's be done with timidity and trifling. Let's get to work preaching the one Book that magnifies Christ, meets the needs of people and matures local churches.

How our country needs a mighty army of preachers who are anointed of God and armed with the Word of God. Someone has rightly said there must be some "pound" in expound, some "expose" in expository and some "reach" in preach. Amen! Let's be the expounding, expository, preaching pastors that local churches so desperately need. Let's not allow our educational foundation to be undermined. Let science bow to Genesis. Let the astronomer pay homage to Job. Let the liberal swallow Jonah. Let the intellectual salute Luke. Let the modern scholar fall at the feet of the peerless pedagogue, Jesus Christ. John Ruskin declared: "The Bible is the Book of God and the god of books." So be it.

Evangelism Based on Biblical Imperatives

Article XIV of the GARBC articles of faith includes the following words: "We believe the true mission of the church is the faithful witnessing of Christ to all men as we have opportunity." Article II of the GARBC constitution is entitled "Purpose" and includes the following words: "to promote the spirit of evangelism; to spread the gospel; to advance Regular Baptist educational and missionary enterprises at home and abroad." Our evangelism must not be based on advertising gimmicks but on Biblical imperatives.

First, *concern* is a Biblical imperative. "But when he saw the multitudes, he was moved with compassion on them, because they fainted, and were scattered abroad, as sheep having no shepherd. Then saith he unto his disciples, The harvest truly is plenteous, but the labourers are few; pray ye therefore the Lord of the harvest, that he will send forth labourers into his harvest" (Matt. 9:36-38). In his great sermon entitled "Travailing for Souls," Charles Haddon Spurgeon used Isaiah 66:8 as an illustrative text: "As soon as Zion travailed, she brought forth her children." Among other things, Spurgeon said: "Why is it that there must be this anxiety before desirable results are gained? For answer it might suffice us to say that God has so appointed. It is the order of nature. The child is not born into the world without the sorrows of the mother, nor is the bread which sustains life procured from the earth without toil. . . . Why, it is so even in ordinary business. We say, 'No sweat, no sweet'; 'no pains, no gains'; 'no mill, no meal.' . . . The power in the hand of God's Spirit for conversions is heart coming into contact with heart. Truth from the heart goes to the heart. This is God's battle-axe and weapon of war in His crusade. He is pleased to use the yearnings, longings and sympathies of Christian men as the means of compelling the careless to think, constraining the hardened to feel and driving the unbelieving to consider. . . . The emotion we feel and the affection we bear are the most powerful implements of soul-winning. God the Holy Spirit usually breaks hard hearts by tender hearts."

How we need concern and compassion for the lost. Tearless theology, sobless singing, painless preaching and compassionless calling are enemies of true evangelism. One of the purposes of the GARBC is "to promote the spirit of evangelism." How we need it! Dry-eyed preachers, hardhearted deacons and prayerless Sunday School teachers have turned many local churches into cold storage areas for sound doctrine. Dr. Bob Jones, Sr., used to say: "It takes evangelistic unction to make orthodoxy function." May we as Regular Baptists lead the way for our fundamentalist brethren in compassionate concern for the lost.

Second, *converts* are Biblical imperatives. We are commissioned in Matthew 28:19 to "make disciples of all nations." Modern evangelism talks a great deal about *decisions;* the Bible speaks of *disciples.* Modern evangelists talk about *commitments;* the Bible refers to *converts.* Paul rejoiced in the

Thessalonian converts who "turned to God from idols to serve the living and true God" (1 Thess. 1:9). Those Thessalonians were converted! They talked, acted and, I am sure, even smelled differently. Paul says, "Therefore if any man be in Christ, he is a new creature: old things are passed away; behold, all things are become new" (2 Cor. 5:17). Baptists believe in a regenerate church membership. Someone has rightly observed that church members who are not individuals of conversion will ultimately be instruments of subversion.

Third, *convictions* are Biblical imperatives of New Testament evangelism. "And so were the churches established in the faith. . ." (Acts 16:5). We must emphasize anew the fulfilling of the Great Commission in all its parts. We are to make disciples, to baptize them and to instruct them. Paul said to Timothy: "But thou hast fully known my doctrine . . ." (2 Tim. 3:10). Preacher, can you say that to your people? Are you the pastor of a Regular Baptist church or do you simply preside over an interdenominational hodgepodge of untaught believers who have never taken a Biblical position? It's a question worth pondering prayerfully. If you have to sacrifice convictions to get crowds, then you ought to be convicted by your crowds. Statistical digitalis is no substitute for sound doctrine. The kind of evangelism that camouflages the offense of the cross is basically dishonest.

Fourth, *churches* are Biblical imperatives of evangelism. Note Acts 16:5 again: "And so were the churches established in the faith, and increased in number daily." The apostle Paul was interested in the establishment of local churches. So must we be! Let us ask God to prosper us in the establishing of hundreds of local churches both here in the United States and around the world. There is at the time of this writing at least one GARBC church in forty-six of our states. We need to plant churches in Alabama, Hawaii, Mississippi and South Carolina. We need to redouble our efforts in the great areas of growth that are mutliplying the metropolitan populations of Houston and Austin, Texas, Washington, D.C., and Phoenix, Arizona. If our worldwide outreach is to expand, we must have more and more local churches in the homeland.

It is not enough just to win converts. They must be baptized, organized and then mobilized. God has provided the instrumentality of the local church to accomplish these purposes. We must ask God for hearts that are compassionate and feet that are shod with the preparation of the gospel of peace.

Ecclesiasticism Based on Biblical Integrity

As we have thought about the great door and effectual that is open before us as an Association, we have touched upon education based upon Biblical inerrancy. That has to do with our *message*. We have touched on evangelism based on Biblical imperatives. That has to do with our *methods*. Now we come to ecclesiasticism based on Biblical integrity. That has to do with our *manners*.

Many years ago I had the privilege of hearing Dr. James McGinley. More than twenty-five years ago he said something that is applicable today. McGinley declared in his unique way: "Now listen, folks, I don't believe that Christ ever came to teach ethics, do you? But I think He was the most ethical gentleman this world has ever known. Do you believe that? And I don't believe that you and I can follow the Lord Jesus Christ and be unethical. He was a gentleman, eh? And I think that while we're standing for the truth and fighting for the truth, let us see to it, my friends, that we are ethical. There are spurious brands of fundamentalism today with which I have no fellowship—they can lie, they can cheat, they can steal, and the Devil himself can't live with them. But they are fundamentalists. I don't want that kind of fundamentalism."

We who are Regular Baptists have a Biblical message and a Biblical methodology which will be enhanced by our practice of Biblical manners. Paul exhorted Titus to "adorn the doctrine of God our Saviour in all things" (Titus 2:10). We must *talk* like Christians. Paul spoke to the Ephesians about "speaking the truth in love" (Eph. 4:15). We must *walk* like Christians. Paul also exhorted the Ephesians that they "henceforth walk not as other Gentiles walk, in the vanity of their mind" (Eph. 4:17). The GARBC has a tremendous Fellowship to offer Bible-believing Baptists. We must get the message to pastors and peoples who are standing for the faith that we will not lower the flag of faith; we will not relax our missionary fervor; we will not grow coldhearted toward evangelism; we will not become weary in well doing. But we will preach the great Baptist distinctives with compassion for the lost and a concern for the autonomy of every local church.

As Baptists, we believe that ecclesiasticism based on Biblical integrity demands respect for the autonomy of each local church. We are not a convention. We are not a denomination with a headquarters. We do not have a college of cardinals; we have a Council of Eighteen. We do not have a national ruler; we have a National Representative. We do not give orders; we provide opportunities. We do not own college or seminary properties; we approve those which hold to our position. We do not own missionary or social agencies; we approve those which will be true to the local churches that hold Regular Baptist positions. We are a *general association.* Some of our Presbyterian and Methodist-oriented fundamentalist friends do not seem to understand our independency at times. But there can be a diversity in our unity, and no true Baptist would ever stand for a Baptist dictator handing down decrees to local churches.

Such respect for local church sovereignty also demands our faithfulness to the Baptist distinctive known as individual soul liberty. Brethren, we are surely big enough in the GARBC to be able to disagree about some things without becoming cantankerous and mean with one another. While we agree on the great doctrines which are our common ground of fellowship, let us be willing to educate each other in some of the debatable areas. Let us be willing to disagree agreeably.

Let us be wise enough to know what is major and what is minor. Let us be wise enough to know what is principle and what is pettiness. Let us be wise enough to know what is Biblical priority and what is personal preference. The GARBC is surely bighearted enough and clearheaded enough to be able to major on the majors and minor on the minors. Biblical inerrancy is major, Biblical inerrancy is primary! Let's not be afraid to debate with each other on other minor issues. Let's not allow ourselves to be intimidated by a fear of Associational ostracism if we speak about textual or so-called "tulip" differences. Remember, Peter learned something by listening to

Paul, and Paul even learned something finally from John Mark.

Ecclesiasticism based on Biblical integrity also demands total separation from unbelief and compromise. Article II of the constitution of the GARBC has to do with our purpose and includes the following words: "to emphasize the Biblical teaching that a breakdown of the divinely established lines between Bible believers and apostates is unscriptural and to be a voice repudiating cooperation with movements which attempt to unite true Bible believers and apostates in evangelistic and other cooperative spiritual efforts."

Some in recent years have endeavored to redefine the practice of separation by dividing it into primary and secondary separations. Such redefinition is not valid for a Regular Baptist. In fact, one major difference between the Conservative Baptist Association and the GARBC is at this point. The Conservative Baptists allow a church to be affiliated with the American Baptist Church (originally known as the Northern Baptist Convention) which permits the presence of apostates, while at the same time receiving that church into the fellowship of the CBA. The founders of the GARBC wisely prohibited such dual affiliation. Biblical separation means no fraternization ecclesiastically with apostates or with those who are believers yet who disobediently work with apostate conventions. An ethical Regular Baptist will not practice Conservative Baptist ecclesiastical polity.

If Joseph M. Stowell was right to maintain the position of Scriptural separation from unbelief, and he was; if Paul R. Jackson was right to maintain an ethical fundamentalism, and he was; if Robert T. Ketcham was right to maintain a militant Regular Baptist position, and he was; if H. O. Van Gilder was right to maintain a theologically sound fundamentalism, and he was; then we must follow faithfully in their train and continue to carry the banner of Biblical separatism into the open and effectual door before us.

An ecclesiasticism based on Biblical integrity is a fundamentalism that is both militant and mannerly. We must earnestly contend for the faith while being ethically courteous to our foes. We must not shirk from the good fight of faith. We must be spiritual gladiators and at the same time conduct ourselves as Scriptural gentlemen. But in a day when Christianity is being assaulted on every side, it is not noble for believers to avoid the conflict by appealing to an unscriptural graciousness or to an innocuous love that will not speak against the enemies of the faith.

There are fundamentalists today who shy away from the separatist position of the GARBC. You may ask: "Are they really fundamentalists?" My answer to your question is that there are basically two kinds of fundamentalism in America today. One is what I call *expedient* fundamentalism. The other I refer to as *obedient* fundamentalism. Expedient fundamentalists believe in *the fundamentals of* the faith, but they do not want to get involved in *the fight for* the faith. They are interested in picking the fruit from fundamentalist orchards, but they are not willing to fight the insidious enemies of the orchards.

Expedient fundamentalists are often irresponsible fundamentalists. They do not seem to relate their Biblical affirmations to their ministerial associations. One such fundamentalist even declared that if a Baptist preacher wanted to invite the pope to his pulpit, it was nobody else's business. He, of course, said it would be unlikely; but if he did it was nobody else's business. Well, I am here to say it is somebody else's business! What you do as a pastor, what you do as a college president, what you do as a missionary agency executive does indeed matter to the whole fundamentalist cause. Whom you invite to speak on your platform says volumes about the seriousness of your dedication to Biblical separation. We must be fundamentalists who realize our responsibility to the whole cause of Scriptural separation from apostasy and compromising evangelicals. It's a matter of Biblical integrity.

Let us be *obedient* fundamentalists. We must be obedient to the Word of God, obedient to the Son of God and, in so doing, obedient to the Spirit of God. Let's not just be crowd builders; let's be local church builders. Let's not just be nominal Baptists; let's be Regular Baptists. Let's not just be separated from apostate denominations; let's be separated from anemic evangelicals who expediently and disobediently want to wear the uniform of fundamentalism without fighting the wars which true fundamentalists have always been willing to fight openly and unashamedly.

"Rise up, O men of God!
Have done with lesser things;
Give heart and soul and mind and strength
To serve the King of kings." *

Rise up, fundamentalists!
The battle rages long;
Unsheath the Spirit's sword
And show the Devil's wrong.

Rise up, separatists!
The Church for you doth wait;
Her purity the holy cause;
Rise up and make her great.

Rise up, Regular Baptists!
Feet with the gospel shod;
As soldiers of the cross of Christ,
Rise up, rise up, O men of God!

* (First stanza from "Rise Up, O Men of God" by William P. Merrill)